the
stress
response

how dialectical behavior therapy

can free you from needless **anxiety, worry,**

anger & other symptoms of stress

CHRISTY MATTA, MA

New Harbinger Publications, Inc.

Publisher's Note

Distributed in Canada by Raincoast Books

Copyright © 2012 by Christy Matta
New Harbinger Publications, Inc.
5674 Shattuck Avenue
Oakland, CA 94609
www.newharbinger.com

Acquired by Melissa Kirk; Cover design by Amy Shoup;
Edited by Elisabeth Beller; Text design by Tracy Carlson

Library of Congress Cataloging-in-Publication Data on file with the publisher

Printed in the United States of America

12 11 10   10 9 8 7 6 5 4 3 2 1   First printing

"Christy Matta has written an elegant description of how dialectical behavior therapy (DBT) concepts relate to everyday stress-related symptoms in peoples' lives. This resonates fully with me, as I and many other practitioners of DBT have found DBT concepts and techniques to be extraordinarily meaningful for ourselves as teachers as well as for those we treat. Her organized and practical examples, exercises, and practice assignments can be helpful for those seeking self-help and clinicians who are seeking a companion text in the course of conducting psychotherapy."

> —Marvin Lew, PhD, ABPP, licensed psychologist and adjunct professor at the Center for Psychological Studies at Nova Southeastern University in Fort Lauderdale, FL

"I personally have found Matta to be grounded, practical, and thoughtful in addressing difficult emotional problems. I am always looking for ways to translate DBT skills to real life and how to apply old material to new contexts. Matta has certainly done this in her book. In addition to providing user-friendly, practical, how-to steps, she offers a beautiful overview of DBT-based material that addresses a wide and flexible spectrum of coping options."

> —Renee Hoekstra, PsyD, licensed clinical psychologist in Boston, MA

"In *The Stress Response,* Matta has done an effective job of explaining complex issues and techniques in ways that can be understood and are helpful to anyone who experiences stressful emotions. She has shown great creativity in adapting DBT skills to develop an excellent resource that provides many strategies for stress management, which are explained through helpful examples and step-by step exercises. I am so appreciative that Matta has given a gift to anyone who experiences a stress response; that is, she has given a gift to everyone. I look forward to recommending this book to clients, colleagues, and friends."

> —Pat Harvey, coach, trainer, consultant, and coauthor of *Parenting a Child Who Has Intense Emotions*

"*The Stress Response* offers the reader great tools for identifying and managing stress. Matta provides important techniques for learning to trust your body and intuition in order to live a calmer, more peaceful life. The mindfulness exercises in particular provide the reader with a way to cope better with everyday anxiety and worry. I highly recommend this book to anyone looking for concrete ways to reduce stress and anxiety in everyday life."

> —Carey Wagner, LICSW, licensed independent clinical social worker

"I am pleased to recommend this book to anyone who is interested in learning to understand and manage stress. In this book, Matta skillfully translates the science of emotion and the stress response into user-friendly, practical skills and techniques that can be applied in a variety of situations that may cause emotional distress. This book will teach readers to become aware of their patterns of response to stressful events, recognize how such reactions can interfere with physical and emotional well-being, and develop specific coping skills to live a more aware, calm, and productive life."

—Michael J. Wagner, PhD, clinician, clinical manager, and director in community behavioral health care

"The core skills of DBT are skills for life. As a DBT therapist, I use these skills every day to live a fully engaged, happy, and healthy life. Matta's straightforward, easy, common-sense approach will not only provide relief from stress and anxiety, but, when practiced on a daily basis, will also enhance your quality of life at work, at play, in relationships, and with your family. I will highly recommend this book to my clients."

—Laura J. Winton, cognitive behavioral/DBT therapist at Washington Hospital Center in Washington, DC

"Matta provides a practical application of research that can help people accept themselves while still striving to improve the way they deal with stress. The book includes examples and exercises that are accessible and engaging. This is a great book for anyone who wants to manage stress better."

—Claire Conry-Murray, PhD, assistant professor of psychology at Penn State University, Beaver

"This book does a wonderful job of translating proven stress-reduction techniques commonly used by therapists into an easy-to-read and practical manual for managing stress in daily life."

—Kristin Neff, PhD, associate professor of human development and culture at the University of Texas at Austin

"Almost every chapter [in *The Stress Response*] includes a situation of a real person, which better helps put the information into perspective and makes it easier for you to relate it to your own life. It shows the journal exercises that each person would use, as well, which I thought was helpful and made the whole thing a lot less confusing.... There are definitely a lot of strategies in this book that I will consider using."

—Katie Wanta, blogger

Contents

Acknowledgments

Many people contributed to this book in both direct and indirect ways. I want to thank my earliest teachers, Silvia Canetto and Wayne Viney, who inspired in me a love of learning and a quest for understanding. Your lessons are included in this book in many ways.

I was introduced to *dialectical behavior therapy* (DBT) at the Bridge of Central Massachusetts, and it is to the Bridge and the many people I worked with there that I owe a deep debt of gratitude. I'd like to thank Doug Watts at the Bridge, who hired me as a manager and gave me the opportunity to grow as both an administrator and a clinician. I owe a deep sense of gratitude to Steve Murphy and Barry Walsh, who first gave me the opportunity to learn, practice, and understand DBT. It is their passion to provide effective treatment and their belief in my abilities that allowed me to master the DBT skills and concepts that are central to this book. Marvin Lew has been a consistent source of support and knowledge, particularly around behavioral and *cognitive behavioral therapy* (CBT) treatment strategies. And to Pat Harvey, who was the first to suggest that I write a book, thank you for your encouragement.

I'd like to thank all the excellent teachers and trainers that I've had in DBT. Charlie Swenson and Cindy Sanderson brought the treatment alive for me, and I owe them a tremendous token of gratitude.

My family and friends have been a major source of support. I am so grateful to have you all in my life. To the most important people in my life—my children, Isabel, Leila, and Adrian, and my husband, Maher—I thank you for the support, patience, and love that made this project possible.

I would like to thank my editors at New Harbinger, who gave me the opportunity to write this book and deserve much credit and appreciation. I'm grateful to Melissa Kirk for her commitment to this book, wise editing, helpful criticism, and practical suggestions. I deeply appreciate the editorial guidance I received from Jess Beebe and her in-depth knowledge of DBT. I also owe a debt of gratitude to Nicola Skidmore and Elisabeth Beller for their thoughtful and helpful editing and to everyone else at New Harbinger.

Introduction

Emotions are complex, but they are not arbitrary. They come and go like waves on the ocean and, like waves, they can be fun and exciting or painful and disorienting. If you don't understand how emotions work, it can feel like you're standing in the ocean with your back to the waves: you can't predict when one is coming or make decisions about how to manage it. If your back is to the waves, you are at the mercy of the sea.

Stress can be both overwhelming and painful. It can leave you tense and unable to think or sleep. Recurrent stress takes a physical toll, causing fatigue and irritability. When you are stressed, you may chronically anticipate the next difficult event.

Without strategies to manage it, the effect of stress on your life can be destructive. Stress is linked to problems with physical health, such as obesity, diabetes, and hypertension, as well as serious mental health problems such as depression, anxiety disorders, and substance abuse.

To reduce stress, you must first learn how your emotions work. This book helps you do the following:

- Understand your stress.

- Begin to see the patterns in how you respond to events and circumstances.

- Recognize the interaction between stressful life events and your response to them.

- Learn to identify early emotional triggers to reduce the stress response.

- Become effective at coping with life events that contribute to stress.

What Is Stress?

The regular use of the term "stress" began during World War I and II with the exploration of the pressures that had an impact on the well-being of soldiers (Lazarus 1999). After the wars, the word was used in the context of pressures at work, school, and home. Today we use the word "stress" to refer to an individual's everyday struggle to adapt to the pressures of life.

According to Richard Lazarus (1999), the concept of stress encompasses both the external forces that contribute to the pressure in an individual's life (such as trauma, conflict, and isolation) and the internal strains that result from stress. This internal strain is often referred to as the *stress response* and has both physiological and emotional components.

In the course of daily life we each encounter social, physiological, and psychological forces that contribute to stress. An increase in external stressful events in daily life contributes to internal physical and emotional strain.

Understanding and coping with stress is complicated by individual differences. Our genetic vulnerability to stress, perceptions of events, and personality factors all contribute to differences in how we experience stress. Stress occurs through a highly individual interaction between a person and environmental events. This book is designed to help you gain understanding of your own response to events, how the interaction of your response with events in life impacts stress, and how to effectively respond to and cope with stress.

Often, when we're stressed, all we want to do is escape—escape how we feel, what we're thinking, the demands being made on us, and who we are. This book will ask you to *focus* on what is happening during times of stress instead of running from it. It might get uncomfortable—for some of us, slowing down and becoming aware of our stress is emotionally painful—but this approach can take us beyond merely surviving from one day to the next. And it's the first step in managing stress symptoms, such as the headaches, tension, and lack of energy of prolonged stress.

What Is an Emotion?

Stress and emotion are two closely linked but separate entities. The experience of emotion has a significant impact on your experience of stress and vice versa. Throughout this book, I will be exploring the relationship between stress and emotion. Knowing how we experience emotion and what brings it about helps us understand our relationships with external stressors.

Although many people feel like emotions just happen or are irrational, emotions actually occur as part of an understandable internal process. This process involves the events in our lives, how we appraise those events, the changes in the brain and body, and our urges to act. Take, for example, the experience of the emotion anger. Anger is not simply a feeling—it's a process. An event—say, getting cut off in traffic—generates an appraisal ("That person is a jerk"). Almost instantaneous body and brain changes occur that might include the tensing of muscles, increased heart rate, a red face, or clenched fists. The urge to act—in this case to shout at the person in the other car—is the final step in this internal emotional process that we label as the experience of anger. The process of emotion will be explored in more detail in chapter 1.

What Is Dialectical Behavior Therapy?

Dialectical behavior therapy (DBT) grew out of the work of Marsha Linehan, Ph.D. (1993a). Linehan, a *cognitive behavioral* psychologist by training, developed the theory while working primarily with women who were suicidal and engaged in self-harming behaviors. Initially, she approached her treatment from a strict cognitive behavioral perspective, which generally would include brief, time-limited therapy in which a therapist would collaborate with a client to identify and change problematic thoughts.

Over time, Linehan found that cognitive behavioral techniques were deficient. She noticed that although many people improved with these techniques, too many others responded to treatment with anger or withdrawal. The adaptations she made to her work to address these shortcomings developed into DBT. DBT preserves the cognitive behavioral focus on working with people to change problem thoughts and behaviors. However, it also emphasizes acceptance and validation strategies designed to recognize the difficulty of change, which can help people stay open to and engaged in the process of change.

Although it was originally designed as an outpatient treatment for women diagnosed with borderline personality disorder, DBT has grown into an effective treatment for people with a wide variety of diagnoses and problems. Its effectiveness in helping people modulate extreme emotions and reduce impulsive and destructive behaviors makes it an attractive treatment, especially for those who struggle with high levels of stress and overwhelming emotion.

Using This Book

Although you might feel overloaded and under constant strain, it is possible to recognize the effects, and, with increased knowledge, change the impact that stress has on your life. Stress and its emotional components occur in an understandable cycle. The DBT approach looks at emotions as part of a story, and it helps to keep this in mind as you consider your own stress, emotion, and the story they tell.

I recommend that you complete the practice exercises as you read the book. Because the information and exercises build upon each other, chapters are most effective if read in order. Although it is possible to skip ahead, completing the earlier exercises makes the entire book more useful. You will also get the most out of the book if you take the time to do each of the exercises. Many of the exercises include writing or recording your experiences; I recommend that you keep a journal or notebook for this purpose, but you can also complete the exercises on blank pieces of loose paper. In DBT, practice is crucial to make any lasting change. The more consistently you do the exercises, the more you will gain from the book.

With DBT, practice exercises and strategies are diverse and varied. Try out different strategies and see what works to reduce your stress levels. It takes practice and repetition to understand and consistently use these skills. I can assure you that when they are practiced over time, people report how helpful they are. For example, the people I've worked with report that DBT skills help them to lead less chaotic lives and to feel less overwhelmed and better able to reach their long-term goals. I invite you to explore the strategies and skills in this book, in the hope that they will help you feel the same.

CHAPTER 1

Understanding Your Stress

Learning how to better handle stress is not about getting rid of all the stress in your life. It is about getting better at determining what's contributing to your problematic stress responses. The goal of this book is to teach you strategies to alleviate severe and prolonged stress and to decrease the anguish and destructive aspects of stress.

In this chapter, you will explore your personal experience of stress. In doing so, you will also examine your emotional reactions to events in your life that are central to the experience of stress. You will gain an understanding of the course of stress, the connection between emotion and stress, and how even stress-related emotions serve a purpose in your life. Finally, you will begin to explore your personal symptoms of stress.

Information, even information about your own internal emotional processes, makes stress more predictable. Predictability is a key factor in reducing the stress response. Many of the activities in this chapter focus on modulating your stress response by learning to predict and label elements of your experience of stress and your stress-related emotions.

The Course of Stress

An occurrence of stress includes the events that trigger a stress response, thoughts that contribute to stress, changes in your body and brain during stress, and your typical behaviors and actions when confronted with stress. Because stress and emotion are so closely linked, it's important to examine your emotional experiences during each of these stages and how stress and your emotional reactions interrelate.

Stressful Events

Stress begins with an event. Something happens. It might be something big and obvious, like a death, divorce, or loss of a job. It might be a daily hassle, such as a rude cashier at the grocery store, the kids spilling juice on a floor you just mopped, the bank making an error in your account, loneliness, a sick pet, or a demanding boss. Or it might be something very small that you don't notice unless you pay close attention, like the smell of a particular aftershave, the buzz of an incoming e-mail, or your heart pounding after a cup of coffee.

Beyond activating a physiological stress response, these events are also the starting point for the process of an emotional experience. Anger, anxiety, guilt, and shame are typical stress-related emotions. You may be aware of some of the stressors in your life but unaware of all the events that trigger the stress response and a stress-related emotional reaction. At times it may seem like your stress comes from everywhere, but it does not.

• *Stacey's Story*

Stacey is a divorced cardiac nurse in her midforties raising two teenaged boys. As a single parent, she is constantly juggling the demands of her career with the demands of raising two sons. Her work is stressful, especially with the downturn in the economy, which has decreased the number of staff on shift. She feels rushed and pressured to complete work by herself that used to be done by several people and frequently stays late to complete her work, then races home to get the boys to after-school activities, oversee homework, and do household chores. Stacey reports always feeling stressed and anxious. In the morning, preparing for work, she begins to worry about her day. She often goes through her morning routine on automatic pilot, barely aware of the process of getting dressed. Her thoughts race about upcoming demands on her time, her inability to meet them, and, ultimately, her personal inadequacies. At night, she can't stop worrying about life-threatening emergencies she's dealt with at work and the possibility that she, herself, might die. She thinks about how fragile life is and worries about what would happen to her children if she died. Stacey spends much of the day anxious, irritable, and feeling isolated in her problems.

PRACTICE: IDENTIFYING TIMES OF STRESS

When you pay attention to those times when you consistently experience stress, you gain valuable information. As you get good at noticing stressful moments, you can begin to ask yourself what you were thinking, doing, or feeling just prior to feeling stressed.

IDENTIFYING A STRESSFUL MOMENT

It's important to begin to recognize when you are feeling stressed.

1. Tune in to times when you are feeling stressed. Become aware of times of the day or situations that tend to leave you on edge, revved up, or highly emotional. Pay particular attention to times when you experience anxiety, anger, and shame, which often occur along with the stress response.

2. Choose three or four times during the day (say in the shower, after a meeting, or before bed) to stop and ask yourself, "Am I stressed?"

3. Pay attention to your symptoms of stress, such as a racing heart, muscle tension, inability to concentrate, worried thoughts, or shaking hands.

4. Make a list in your journal of times during the day that you felt stressed.

In Stacey's case, she initially felt she was stressed all the time. After practicing identifying stressful moments, she began to recognize that there were some specific triggers for her stress response: for instance, when she felt particularly pressured at work and had to stay late or when she'd worked with certain colleagues who were unsupportive.

7

Thoughts

What you think about the events in your life matters. Thoughts are a part of your emotional experience and can either tone down or intensify your physiological stress response. Even when you are unaware of them, you have thoughts about what is happening in your life. The content of these thoughts—for instance, perceptions of threats, worries about demands, assessments that events are harmful to you, and anticipation of problems—are often immediate and unintentional. These kinds of appraisals make a significant difference in your stress response (Lazarus 1999).

Here are some thoughts you might have shortly after a favorite coworker is laid off. The event doesn't change, but each possible thought triggers a different set of emotions, which has an impact on whether you experience the event as stressful:

- "Why her? Nobody is safe if she was laid off."

- "It should have been me."

- "I'm next."

- "They don't appreciate anyone here."

- "I can't handle the extra workload with her gone."

- "I'm anxious for her, but this is an opportunity for me."

- "She'll land on her feet. Everything happens for a reason."

- "Change is inevitable. I'll just roll with it."

So the thought you have when a coworker is laid off could trigger confusion, despair, shame, panic, resolve, relief, or excitement. Thoughts that trigger painful and intense emotions will increase your experience of stress.

PRACTICE: IDENTIFYING THOUGHTS DURING STRESS

At this point, you want simply to become aware of the thoughts that are contributing to your stress response. This awareness will help you start to explore the interaction between your internal process and environmental stressors. You'll start by identifying thoughts you have when you are relatively calm and then you'll practice identifying them when you're stressed.

NOTICING YOUR THOUGHTS DURING CALM MOMENTS

1. First become aware of your thoughts during moments of calm. Try to remember to do this exercise in moments when you don't feel particularly stressed (e.g., during your lunch break, while relaxing before bed, or in any moment when you don't need to be anywhere or do anything right away). Do this exercise as often as you wish for several days.

2. Sit quietly and calm yourself by noticing the natural flow of your breath. Become aware of thoughts as they enter your mind. Whom or what are you thinking about? Initially you might find yourself thinking about this exercise. Just notice those thoughts. As thoughts come into your mind, try to notice them quickly, before they become a train of thought and you're swept off into elaborations and associations. Allow the thoughts to come and go like waves on the ocean, without judging or getting attached to them.

3. After two to three minutes of noticing your thoughts, stop and write in a journal or on a piece of paper what you have noticed, using one or two words for each thought, and then write down what you noticed about your thoughts. Were they racing or calm? How did they come into your head? Did they seem to bubble up from nowhere, or was it more like a river of thoughts rushing through your mind?

4. Whenever you remember to, take a moment, again, to notice your thoughts when you feel relatively calm and see whether you can identify how your thinking process works. Are there times when your thoughts seem more calm and others when they seem to race? Do your thoughts repeat? Do you tend to focus more on certain ideas or topics?

NOTICING YOUR THOUGHTS DURING STRESSFUL MOMENTS

[handwritten note in margin: Don't judge these thoughts as being good or...]

1. After you've practiced noticing thoughts during calm moments three or four times, choose a moment when you feel stressed and bring your attention to your thoughts during that time. Don't try to alter what you're thinking. Just watch your thoughts go by. Again notice whom or what you are thinking about. It's normal to find yourself getting caught up in a train of thoughts. When you notice this happening, bring your mind back to the original thought and simply attend to new thoughts as they occur. If this is difficult, it may help to refocus by taking a few deep breaths.

2. Keep the practice to two to three minutes. When you are finished, write down any thoughts you've noticed. How did you experience your thoughts? Did they seem to be racing or jumpy? What did you tend to focus on? How was this experience different than in the first exercise?

   Initially it can be very difficult to notice your own thoughts without getting swept up in them, especially when you're emotional or under stress, so if this exercise was difficult to do, it's okay. With practice, you will be able to step back and watch your thinking without engaging in your thoughts. Start making it a habit to check in with your thoughts when you're stressed.

3. After you've done this practice a few times, look back on your notes and see whether you can discern a pattern. Is there a type of thought you seem to have more often when you're stressed than when you're calm? Is there a topic your thoughts seem to focus on? Do your thoughts seem more urgent when you feel stressed, or do they have a critical tone? In Stacey's case, her thoughts during times of stress were often self-critical (*I'm not a good mother*) or focused on her sons' well-being (*What if both boys hate me, what if they get into drugs, what if they're ostracized because we have less money than their friends?*) or focused on pressures at work (*The workload is unrealistic. I'm helpless to change it, but I need the money and can't leave. I'm trapped*).

   You will use your notes from chapter 2 to discern thought patterns, identify automatic stress-related thoughts, and uncover the meanings attributed to your thoughts, so be sure to write down what you've observed.

Remember, gathering information about your internal reactions to stressors reduces the intensity of your stress. Understanding your stress-related emotions is like turning around and facing the waves in the ocean. They might still be big, but at least you know they're coming.

Stress-Related Body and Brain Changes

Stress is a reaction that happens in both your body and your brain. Your first hint that you're feeling stress is often a change in your body. For example, a pen shakes when you sign a document, you suddenly feel hot and flushed, or you can't stop sweating. This is your body reacting to the perception of a threat and the accompanying emotions of fear or anger.

The human stress response is activated by physical threats—like your car skidding off the road—and psychological and social threats—like a supervisor criticizing your work (Sapolsky 2004; Lazarus 1999). Humans are unique—we can perceive both a growling tiger and a snarky comment by a colleague as threatening.

Your physiological stress response is a reaction to both immediate threats and the anticipation of stress. Let's say your teenaged son is out past curfew; this is not an immediate threat. First you're irritated at his disregard for rules, and then you wonder why he hasn't called. You reject cell phone problems as unreasonable and arrive at a panicked conclusion that he's had an accident. Your physiological response to the anticipation of a stressor (he's had an accident) is the same as if the stressor was a reality and requiring you to react. It doesn't matter that your teenager strolls in fifteen minutes later claiming a dead phone battery. The worst has not happened. You are not required to act. But your anticipation has already activated the pounding heart and high blood pressure of a stress response. The only difference between anticipating a stressful event and being faced with an immediate stressor is the intensity of the response.

ACUTE STRESS

In times of stress, the brain coordinates changes throughout the body (McEwen 2007; Sapolsky 2004). To understand the immediate stress response, it's helpful to remember that it originally developed to provide your muscles with extra amounts of energy and powers of exertion.

The body's response to acute stress is a mobilization for emergency. According to Robert Sapolsky, during acute stress, your body shuts down activities that support long-term survival, like digestion and cell repair, and activates systems that immediately support short-term survival (Sapolsky 2004).

The brain releases *chemical mediators* (molecules involved in transmitting information from one cell to another) such as *adrenaline* that help you respond to the stressor. When you perceive something as stressful, these chemical mediators increase heart rate and blood pressure, enhancing the delivery of oxygen and sugar to your muscles for rapid energy use.

The brain and body produce many amazing changes in response to acute stress. Certain aspects of memory improve. Your senses become sharper. Your perception of pain can become blunted. A tired and nasally congested man driving in a snowstorm will become alert, be able to breathe clearly, and react quickly when his tires slip on the road. A mother won't notice the pain of a sprained ankle as she pulls her child out of oncoming traffic. We've all had these moments of sudden clarity and physical proficiency. They can occur anywhere, at any time, and they focus your thoughts, sharpen your senses, and give you strength to quickly react to danger.

However, if your acute stress is a response to a psychological stressor (for instance, getting bad news in an e-mail while at work), you may not have a physical outlet for the extra energy associated with your acute stress response. It is often the *unreleased* energy of a stress response that contributes to some of the most uncomfortable symptoms of stress, such as jitteriness, pounding heart, shaking, and trembling.

WEAR AND TEAR ON THE BODY

Whether it's noise, pollution, sleep deprivation, a poorly lit work environment, illness, or a lack of control over your workday, repeated stresses in daily life can make you sick. According to Robert Sapolsky, with repetitive and prolonged activation, the stress response can become more damaging than the stressor itself (Sapolsky 2004).

Living in a constant state of emergency causes you to tire more quickly. If your body is always preparing for urgent action, it's unable to also take care of longer-term needs. Urgency requires your body to shut down activities necessary for long-term survival and enhances those high-priority mechanisms that produce immediate energy and action. Longer-term functions, such as digestion, growth, reproduction, tissue repair, sex drive, and immune function are all affected by repeated episodes of stress (that is, *chronic stress*) (Sapolsky 2004; Miller, Cohen, and Ritchie 2002).

Robert Sapolsky points to cardiovascular disease as a clear example of stress wearing on the body (Sapolsky 2004). Psychological stress affects the body in the same way as a physical threat, but often there is no physical release of energy. You might be standing in line or sitting in your car, but your body still elevates its blood pressure and heart rate in response to stress. Blood coursing through your veins under high amounts of pressure causes damage over time. Once damaged, blood vessels can become inflamed. Under stress, the heart pounds away at increased rates. The increased pressure of blood entering the heart and the long-term exertion can cause damage to the heart. This damage in the heart and inflammation of the veins are currently the best predictors of cardiac risk (Sapolsky 2004).

A chronic stress burden can impact brain structure and your behavior, and it may accelerate aging of the brain (McEwen 2007). Prolonged stress can result in losses of cognitive functioning and impairments in memory. In a recent study, heightened stress was shown to actually rewire the brain to promote habitual cycles of stress (Dias-Ferreira et al. 2009). With pro-longed stress, structural and functional changes affect how the brain works, possibly in the areas of decision-making and goal-directed behavior.

STRESS AND ILLNESS

Both Bruce McEwen (2007) and Robert Sapolsky (2004) discuss the role of stressors in the development of illness. Stressors do not necessarily make you sick. But they do increase your risk of getting diseases. They also increase the risk that once you have a disease, a compromised immune system will leave your body less able to fight infection and your defenses will be overwhelmed.

Repeatedly turning on your stress response or being unable to turn it off can have complex consequences. Prolonged stress plays a role in the development of a number of health issues, including diabetes, obesity, and hypertension (McEwen 2007). Evidence suggests that repetitive stress has an impact on mood, anxiety disorders, chronic pain, and our ability to control food intake. Psychological distress plays a role in advancing the symptoms of pain disorders, such as fibromyalgia and mandibular joint disorder (McEwen 2007). Chronic burnout, which is characterized by emotional or physical exhaustion, lowers work productivity and heightens feelings of depersonalization, lack of satisfaction, and low self-esteem; it's also associated with an increased risk of type 2 diabetes (Melamed et al. 2006).

Once you have an illness, reducing stress doesn't simply make the illness go away or reverse the wear and tear on the body. But the good news is that the effects of prolonged stress on the brain appear to be reversible. *Neuroplasticity*—your brain's ability to change as a result of your experiences—allows you to negate much of the damage of long-term stress. Lifestyle changes and changes in habitual thought patterns can reverse many of the mental and psychological effects of recurrent or chronic stress.

PRACTICE: NOTICING YOUR BODY'S PHYSICAL STATE

What's happening within your body can be much like music that is playing in the background while you go about your day. When you're engrossed in other things, it's easy to take no notice of it. But if you bring your attention to it, you suddenly realize that it has been there all along.

1. Choose times during the day to scan your body for signs of stress. You might choose moments that you know are typically stressful or highly emotional for you or you can choose regular intervals throughout your day, such as when you arise in the morning, during your lunch break, and when you go to bed at night, checking in and noticing whether you are feeling stressed.

2. Take one to two minutes to scan your body. Start at the top of your head. Notice any muscle tension, aches and pains, movement, or other sensations such as shaking or tingling. Slowly move your attention down your body, taking note as you go of signs of tension. Bring your attention from your head to your neck, shoulders, and torso. Next notice your arms and hands, hips, legs, and feet.

Remember, the acute stress response frequently includes heart pounding, light-headedness, dizziness, and muscle tension, while fatigue and lack of energy are signs that your body has been using up all its resources in emergency mode.

3. Jot down in a journal or log (a) where in your body you noticed uncomfortable physical responses (for example you might write that you noticed it in your neck and hands) and (b) what sensations you noticed (for example, muscle tension and shakiness).

When you're stressed, it's particularly important to become aware of what is happening within your body. Your body is always available to provide you with information. Noticing what's happening in your body gives you a greater opportunity to recognize signs of stress early and manage your stress levels.

Behavioral Urges

Emotions can be differentiated from each other by how they influence your thinking, by how your body is responding to them, and by how they impact your urge to act or behave (Roseman, Wiest, and Swartz 1994). Fear, for example, is associated with an urge to flee. In contrast, happiness is associated with urges to smile, share, and hug. With DBT we learn that each emotion has one or more corresponding urges to act (Linehan 1993b).

FIGHT OR FLIGHT

The emotional components of a typical stress response are connected with a particular set of urges to act. Most people have heard of the fight-or-flight response. This is nature's way of ensuring the survival of the human race. Fight and flight were critical responses to stress when our ancestors' survival depended on the ability to fight off attacking tribes or flee from dangerous animals.

Today, however, stress is more likely triggered by work deadlines, a traffic jam, a harried lifestyle, health problems, or layoffs than by a pack of hungry wolves. But the fight-or-flight urge is the same. If you are unprepared for a meeting, those desires to sink into the floor or fake an urgent phone call are escape urges. The desire to shout and curse at traffic or punch someone are stress-related fight urges.

Stacey has the urge to escape from her problems. She overeats to distract herself from self-criticism and avoids addressing any health issues that would confirm her fears of dying.

WOMEN AND THE BEHAVIORAL URGE

There is evidence to suggest that in addition to the fight-or-flight response to stress, women may have another set of behavioral urges. Like our male ancestors, females had to flee from danger and fight for survival. But females also had to ensure the survival of children. Shelley Taylor and colleagues (2000) suggest that a different set of hormones and some differences in physiology make women respond to some stress with the urge to *tend and befriend*: when stressed, women are likely to have the urge to care for their loved ones and to seek social affiliation.

Like the fight-or-flight response, tend and befriend is an adaptive urge based on action. Unlike fight or flight, tending and befriending has more to do with ensuring survival by protecting the young and creating supportive social networks than running from predators or fighting for food.

PRACTICE: NOTICING THE BEHAVIORAL URGE

The purpose of this exercise is to help you to become aware of impulses or inclinations to act that are a part of your emotional experience. What you actually do might be consistent with your impulse or quite different. For example, you might have the urge to flee from an important presentation at work but show up at the appointed time and make the presentation anyway. It's important to begin to understand your impulses to act, and this exercise can help you get started:

1. The next time you're stressed, pay attention both to what you feel like doing and to how you actually behave. You may need to calm yourself with a few deep breaths first so you can slow down and observe your internal process. Notice if you become short-tempered or irritable with the people around you. Watch for the

common stress-related behavioral urges: notice when you tend to want to escape, have the urge to fight, or reach out to and care for others. If it's too difficult to do while you're stressed, think back to a time in the past few days or week when you felt stressed and try to remember what you wanted to do.

2.   Try not to judge your urges as either "good" or "bad." Your urges to act may cause you problems, but they can also be helpful and protective.

3.   Write in your journal what you felt like doing in that moment and what you actually did do.

4.   Repeat the exercise over the next several days. Do you notice any patterns emerging? Are your urges different when you feel threatened than when you feel overburdened? Does anger prompt a different urge than anxiety or disappointment?

What we feel like doing may very well be what is called for in a given situation; however, our urges to act may also be inadequate or even problematic in certain circumstances. For example, the fight response might not be the most effective reaction to the stress that's triggered by a traffic jam or the restaurant getting your order wrong. It's essential to understand your urges to act in order to learn to apply healthy stress-management strategies.

PRACTICE: CREATING A STRESS LOG

Creating a record of your stress experiences will give you valuable information. Memory, especially of thoughts and events that accompany intense emotion, is often inaccurate. A record that you complete regularly is the best way to get accurate information about the frequency and intensity of your stress response.

The exercise above showed you how to get started. Now take a journal or notebook and create a log with seven rows, labeled as in the sample table below. If you complete the log once a day for a week, you should gain some valuable information about how stress operates for you.

The following is an example of Stacey's stress log.

Date and time	*May 15, 3:00 p.m.*
Intensity of stress (on a scale of 1–5)	*4*
First awareness of stress response	*I first realized I was stressed when I started becoming irritable and short-tempered with coworkers.*
Prompting event	*Joan called in sick, which meant I'd have to work late and miss Joe's track meet*
Thoughts	*This place doesn't support its workers. Joe's going to hate me. I never follow through for him.*
Body response	*Tense, clenched jaw*
Urge to act	*Fight—strike out at coworkers*

Here are some specifics on filling out your log:

- *Date and time.* Once a day, write down when, over the course of the day, you've felt stressed or anxious. Write down the date and time. Simply beginning to log the times when you have stress will give you important information.

- *Intensity of stress.* Rate the level of stress you experience. Is it as bad as it ever gets—a 5—or are you anxious and jittery, stuck in negative thoughts but still functioning—a 3—or is it a mild nervousness that's distracting but manageable—a 1?

- *First awareness of stress response.* It's important to become aware of when in your stress story you notice that you are stressed. Write down when you first notice stressful thoughts, such as when your voice cracks during a big meeting. Also write about stress-related urges or behaviors such as feeling like cursing your boss or crying in the bathroom of a restaurant.

- *Prompting event.* Where did the stress and anxiety start? What set it off? If you're not sure, take a wild guess. What happened right before you became stressed? Over time, you'll begin to get a better idea.

- *Thoughts.* Tune in to your thoughts. What's running through your mind? If your mind is a radio station, what song is it playing?

- *Body response.* Write down in what part of your body you noticed the stress response and what the response was. Do you feel tense in your shoulders, are you clenching your jaw, or do you feel dread in the pit of your stomach?

- *Behavioral urge.* What do you feel like doing—fleeing, hiding, hurting someone, hurting yourself, calling your mom? Write it down.

You will be able to use this information in exercises later in this chapter and throughout the book. Doing so will help you learn how to reduce both the frequency and the intensity of the stress you feel. With this record, you will put together the thoughts, behaviors, and actions associated with stress. Patterns will emerge. What triggers stress and how you respond to stress will become more predictable rather than incomprehensible.

Experiencing Stress

When you break down the components of stress, you can see that each feature occurs in a logical sequence.

However, your sensitivity to stress and your emotional vulnerability may further complicate your response. Genetic factors, experiences early in life, physical health, and difficulty altering perceptions of stressful events all increase your vulnerability to stress (McEwen 2007; Sapolsky 2004).

Your Sensitivity to Stress

Genetic and health factors may make you more susceptible to stress. A person with a predisposition to hypertension, for example, will experience more extreme stress-related increases in blood pressure and heart rate than the average person. This person will experience the physical symptoms of stress—pounding heart, light-headedness, nausea—more acutely and for a longer period of time than someone who does not have hypertension.

Our experiences in early life have effects on physiology and behavior. Childhood experiences affect how you view the world and your thoughts and beliefs about your own capabilities. Traumatic early experiences can shape how you respond to stressors and make you more vulnerable to having intense reactions to potentially stressful events.

A vulnerability to stress also has an impact on the intensity and length of your experience of stress. Compared to the stress experience of the average person, your stress may be any or all of the following:

- More easily triggered

- Stronger and more extreme

- Longer lasting

If you're sensitive to stress, a small event that others might overlook or quickly move past is more likely to trigger emotion for you. Once triggered, the emotion tends to be extreme. Instead of apprehension, you experience panic. If you're stress-sensitive, your feelings take longer to dissipate. When you're already highly emotional, you're more likely to be overwhelmed by emotion and stressed by new circumstances (Linehan 1993a).

Your perceptions, lifestyle, and health have a significant impact on your stress response. Fortunately you can change how you think about stressful life events as well as how you typically respond to stress. You can make changes to your lifestyle and influence your health to decrease your sensitivity to stress. Exploring your individual stress story will help provide you with information about how stress works for you and improve your response to stress, whether you're someone who tends to be sensitive to stress and anxiety or are simply experiencing a great deal of stress now. You will be able to use this information throughout the book, as strategies are introduced to help you weather stressful times.

The Aftereffects of Stress

The stressful event is over and your stress has passed, so you should be back to normal, right? Unfortunately, it doesn't always work this way. The event that triggered your stress may be over and you may not even be thinking about it anymore, but your body hasn't returned to equilibrium.

Immediately after the stress has passed, the energy expenditure and changes in your body from the stress response impair your ability to do these things:

- Perform tasks.

- Tolerate frustration.

- Resolve cognitive conflict.

- Help others.

Exposure to an environmental stressor that requires effort and demands attention results in cognitive fatigue. Following an occurrence of such stress, you're more likely to have restricted attention and to neglect social cues. For example, say you've just nailed an important presentation at work. The stress is gone. You may be singing along to a favorite song on the radio, but when you pull out of the parking lot, you get into a fender bender. In this case, your ability to bring your full attention to the task of driving was still impaired by the stress you had previously experienced. In another example, imagine you've been caring for a colicky baby who has been crying all day. In the evening, the baby may have finally calmed and slept. But after the stress of the day, you neglect cues that your partner is worried about your finances and you fail to notice that your mother is sounding depressed on the phone. Even when your experience of stress is over, narrowed attention makes it difficult to think clearly, problem solve, or respond to and help the people around you. The stress might be over, but the effects still linger.

The Connection between Stress and Emotion

Certain emotions, such as jealousy, anger, anxiety, shame, and fear, often occur in response to stressful events (Lazarus 1999). Other emotions, such as happiness, excitement, and love, which are typically considered positive emotions, can still be linked to the experience of stress. A promotion or new baby might elicit feelings of joy and, at the same time, create life strain and stress.

Often the most distressing part of the stress response is experiencing the painful and intense emotions triggered by stressful events. These emotions are central to the experience of stress-related symptoms. For example anger, sadness, and anxiety increase *rumination* (going over an experience again and again in your mind) while aggravation, hostility, nervousness, and fear can interfere with your ability to focus.

To better understand and cope with your stress, it's essential that you understand your emotions. Learning to identify and name emotions, and to understand why you are having an emotion and how your thinking can alter your emotions, can help you cope. A greater understanding of your emotional experience increases your sense of control and reduces emotional intensity and reactivity, thereby reducing stress.

Naming Your Emotions

Applying a verbal label to how you're feeling can give you a sense of control over your emotion and decrease its intensity. According to Robert Plutchik, emotions can be organized into categories with about eight basic emotions that all people experience (Plutchik 1980). All other emotions are some combination of basic emotions. We are all born with the capacity to feel joy, trust, anger, sorrow, surprise, disgust, anticipation, and fear. Feelings like fondness and caring would be associated with joy, while disappointment and loneliness are related to sorrow.

Stress is most closely connected to the basic emotions of fear and anger. Like fear or anger, the stress response is triggered by the perception of a threat and prompts the fight-or-flight response. The physical responses of breathlessness, tense muscles, and sweating are related to the feelings of apprehension, dread, nervousness, worry, panic, and shock.

Other emotions are also linked with stress and anxiety. The fatigue, irritability, demoralization, and hostility that define chronic stress are associated with the basic emotions of sorrow and anger. Shame and guilt frequently come with thoughts about losing something important, which triggers stress and anxiety. Below is a table with the eight primary emotions and examples of other emotions that are related. As you familiarize yourself with the emotions in this table you will be better able to articulate your emotional experience.

Related Emotions

Joy	Trust	Anger	Sorrow
Serenity	Admiration	Annoyance	Pensiveness
Ecstasy	Acceptance	Rage	Grief
Optimism	Tolerance	Contempt	Remorse
Cheerfulness	Warmth	Hostility	Demoralization
Love		Envy	Disappointment
Caring		Fury	Sadness

Surprise	Disgust	Anticipation	Fear
Distraction	Boredom	Interest	Terror
Amazement	Loathing	Vigilance	Apprehension
Astonishment	Shame	Awe	Anxiety
Uncertainty	Guilt	Curiosity	Irritability
	Humiliation		Nervousness

It's important to remember that an emotion name is a label we apply to a process that includes events, thoughts, body sensations, and behavioral urges. If you're having trouble naming your emotion, it may help to reflect on each aspect of the process and ask yourself, *What triggered my feelings, what thoughts am I thinking, how is my body responding, and what do I feel like doing?* Exploring the entire process of an emotion may make it easier to find a name for it.

The Purpose of Emotion

An emotion can be neutral—a body response that we simply have to tolerate—or damaging—so intensely painful that it interferes with your ability to live your life and achieve your goals. Worry that a child might be abducted can cause you to isolate him from friends and limit normal and adaptive independence. Fear of public humiliation might cause you to turn down a job at which you'd excel but which would require frequent public presentations. Anxiety about germs and colds can cause you to avoid public spaces and fun group activities.

But an emotion can also be useful. Anxiety about an upcoming deadline or project can motivate you to begin work on it. Worry about a sick child can give you the energy to stay up all night to monitor her fever. Concern for a friend will cause you to go out in a rainstorm to help change a flat tire.

The emotional components of the stress response have important functions. Emotions such as fear, frustration, and sadness can communicate information more quickly and effectively than verbal communication. These emotions also tell us something about ourselves. Marsha Linehan describes three primary functions of any emotion: to elicit actions, to convey feelings and thoughts, and to confirm our own perceptions of the world (Linehan 1993b).

EMOTION ELICITS ACTION

Life pressures that contribute to stress activate a physiological response that impels people to act. We're not usually faced with wild animals, but the fight-or-flight response still has adaptive qualities. The emotions triggered by stressful events also motivate action. Anger can push you to persist in the face of obstacles. Apprehension can keep you out of bad neighborhoods and out of cars with drunk drivers. Anxiety about failure can motivate you to study for a professional certification or prepare for a difficult task. The fear of getting caught can stop you from cutting corners at work or shoplifting. Love and affection motivate you to care for others, ensuring that those who are sick and vulnerable aren't left alone.

EMOTION CONVEYS FEELINGS AND THOUGHTS TO OTHERS

Words are essential, but body language and emotion are often quicker and more influential as communicators. The tremble in your voice when you talk about your mother's illness will communicate, better than your words, your fear and anxiety. People tend to respond to the body language of emotional communication more than to verbal communication. A friend who hears a tremor in your voice may offer support and comfort, while one who hears you calmly state that you're anxious about your mother's next doctor's appointment may not realize the degree of your worry.

EMOTION CONFIRMS SELF-PERCEPTIONS

Emotions not only communicate to other people but also send messages to you. Your body and mind are always receiving and processing information, some of which is not in the forefront of your awareness. The occurrence of an emotion—say, nervousness—can validate your interpretations and experiences. Nervousness confirms an interpretation that *This is important and scary* and authenticates your experience of an important moment.

Symptoms of Stress

The symptoms listed in the next sections are common ones that stressed-out people experience. They are based on the physiological stress response and included here because they are frequently reported symptoms of stress. The list is not intended to be all-inclusive or diagnostic. Rather it is intended to help you identify what you might be experiencing in your own stress story.

PRACTICE: WHAT ARE YOUR STRESS SYMPTOMS?

Write in your journal or on a blank piece of paper symptoms that you commonly experience when stressed.

PHYSICAL SYMPTOMS

Symptoms Linked to Raised Blood Pressure	
Headache	Vomiting
Dizziness	Chest pain
Blurred vision	Shortness of breath
Nausea	

Symptoms Linked to Increased Heart Rate	
Regular or irregular pounding of the heart	Palpitations that can be felt in the chest, throat, or neck
Conscious, unpleasant awareness of your own heartbeat	Palpitations felt with emotions such as excitement or fright
Sensation of skipped or stopped beats	

Other Physical Symptoms	
Jitteriness	Sweating
Nervousness	Wobbly legs
Shaking	Crying
Trembling	Irritation
Enhanced memory	Tiredness
Memory problems	Loss of appetite
Tenseness	Disinterest in sex
Energy	Sleep problems
Feeling like you need to move	Tightness in jaw
Dryness in your mouth	Clenched teeth
Feeling touchy	Lower-back pain
Feeling hot and flushed	Heavy feeling in arms or legs

PSYCHOLOGICAL SYMPTOMS

Worry	
Feeling close to panic	Worrying that you are going crazy
Being overwhelmed by worry	Being frightened by physical symptoms like shakiness or faintness
Being unable to distract yourself from worries	Worrying that you'll have a heart attack
Worrying that you'll hurt or offend people	Worrying that you might be mentally ill
Thinking that life is meaningless	Worrying about making mistakes

Trouble Focusing	
Difficulty keeping your mind on task	Having bad dreams
Difficulty controlling your thoughts	Having your mind go blank
Staying stuck in unpleasant thoughts that you can't get rid of	Difficulty making decisions
Reviewing past events, conversations, and actions repetitively	

Self-Judgment	
Calling yourself names	Feeling worthless and inferior to others
Comparing yourself to others and considering yourself inadequate	Lacking satisfaction in your personal accomplishment
Thinking of yourself as a failure	Having low self-esteem

Emotional Symptoms	
Moodiness	Unhappiness
Extreme fluctuation in emotions	Loneliness
Irritability	Sadness
Short-temperedness	Feeling overwhelmed
Inability to relax	

BEHAVIORAL SYMPTOMS AND THE AVOIDANCE URGE

It's common to respond to high levels of stress with a desire to avoid painful emotions, demands from others, new experiences, situations that feel threatening, and other stress-related circumstances. But if stress is recurrent for you, you may avoid rather than approach situations that, although stressful, are important to living a fulfilling life.

Attempts to manage extreme and painful emotion by steering clear of stressful situations can turn into problems themselves. And problems can multiply if you avoid the painful emotions these situations provoke by engaging in unhealthy or risky behaviors such as drinking alcohol excessively, engaging in self-harm, using substances, neglecting your responsibilities, over- or undereating, sleeping too much, being physically violent, and having trouble relating in healthy ways with friends and family.

Simply steering clear of all reminders of and thoughts about stressful events can also cause problems. You don't want to hear criticism from your supervisor, so you avoid contact. Your sister's cancer worries you, so you don't talk about it. You've been dizzy and having pains in your stomach, so you ignore them. The desire to avoid criticism from a supervisor taken to an extreme might mean covering up a mistake that has dire consequences. For some people, repeated attacks of intense fear and anxiety can result in an avoidance of most activities outside the home.

Like many things in life, this urge to avoid stressful situations becomes problematic when it causes you to avoid important life events, becomes your default response, or leads to unhealthy or risky behaviors.

MAKING SENSE OF YOUR STRESS SYMPTOMS

Your symptoms of stress are individual and tell you a lot about your own stress story. Take note of the symptoms you've written down from the list above. Whether symptoms are problematic and chronic varies for each individual. Signs that stress is problematic for you include the following:

- Losing a sense of control over your symptoms (for example if you can't stop worrying, can't concentrate, or are unable to calm down)

- Having prolonged and recurrent symptoms that continue for weeks or months

- Having symptoms that interfere with your daily functioning, such as avoiding certain people or avoiding paying bills

- Experiencing negative emotion and emotional exhaustion that lasts for days or weeks

- Having frequent physical exhaustion or dangerous physical symptoms, such as chronically high blood pressure (such symptoms should be checked by a physician to ensure there is not an underlying medical cause)

- Repeatedly acting in ways that are risky or may cause health problems, such as overeating or drinking alcohol excessively in response to stress

Psychological distress, physical threats, and difficult social circumstances all activate the same stress response. The symptoms can range from mild to severe and might cause little or no disruption in your life or could be severely debilitating. Gaining a greater understanding of the symptoms of your stress will help you use the strategies in this book to manage problematic and chronic stress.

Wrap-Up

In this chapter you began to explore the relationship between the external stressors in your life and your stress response. By completing the practice exercises, you started to investigate your own internal process of experiencing stress and emotion as well as the interaction between your internal experience of stress and external stressors. Identifying your thoughts, body responses, and urges to act that are related to the stressful events in your life helps make your stress response more predictable. With predictability, the stress response becomes smaller. At the same time, by completing the exercises in this chapter you gain valuable information about your individual experience of stress. With greater self-knowledge you are better able to choose ways of responding to your stress that are effective for you.

CHAPTER 2

Unwinding Your Mind

In the previous chapter, you saw that your thoughts play an integral role in your experience of stress and anxiety. What you *think* about the events that happen in your life, more than the actual events themselves, may determine how much stress you experience. Beliefs shape our expectations of the world. These beliefs—such as the belief that a social situation is threatening or that anything less than perfection is failure—have a significant effect on whether an event will trigger a stress response. The exact same stressors, perceived and evaluated by two different people, will affect each person differently (Sapolsky 2004).

In the 1950s and 1960s, Albert Ellis and Aaron T. Beck looked at how thoughts contribute to problems with emotions and behaviors (Ellis and Harper 1975; Beck et al. 1979). These early works serve as a foundation for DBT's focus on thoughts that precede intense emotional reactions.

How Thoughts Can Contribute to Stress

Each of us has a set of beliefs, expectations, rules, and interpretations that we use to make sense of the world. These are a result of cognition and past experiences. Some of these are very helpful as we go through life. They serve us well in forming relationships, getting through the workday, achieving goals, and finding purpose in life. Others are distorted, rigid, or exaggerated. They interfere with our ability to accurately remember events, lead us to misinterpret the present, and keep us stuck in intense stress and anxiety.

Normal stress and anxiety is a response to a realistic danger. The danger may be a physical threat, such as a hooded stranger in a dark alley, or a social threat, such as gossip that will damage your reputation at work. Stress from a realistic threat dissipates once the danger has passed. You safely get into your car or you talk directly to your coworkers and stop the gossip.

Abnormal anxiety is a greatly disproportionate reaction that lasts even when no danger exists (Beck and Emery 2005). It's important to understand that some thoughts are accurate appraisals of the world around us, while others are exaggerated or distorted.

Everyone exaggerates problems and gets stuck in worries sometimes. There is no magic line that defines a "normal" versus "abnormal" amount of worry and distortion. And it is not necessary or even particularly helpful to label yourself as either normal or abnormal. What does help is to begin to identify those thoughts that are faulty and that needlessly intensify your stress and anxiety. In this chapter, you will learn about the following:

- The concepts of dialectical thinking

- Observing the content of your thoughts

- Evaluating and changing problematic thinking

Dialectical Thinking—Shifting Your Worldview

We will start looking at your thoughts by reviewing a few basic principles. *Dialectics* is a method of argument in which two or more people with different views seek truth through the rational exchange of viewpoints. It is not intended to prove one viewpoint right and another wrong but is an attempt to find how both viewpoints might exist and hold truth simultaneously. In the development of DBT, Marsha Linehan based her theory on a dialectic worldview (Linehan 1993a).

Dialectical thinking attempts to understand how seeming opposites have commonalities and are, despite appearing to be mutually exclusive, in fact, parts of a whole. "Dialectical thinking" might mean accepting that you feel alone at the same time that you are surrounded by people. It might mean doing the best you can while at the same time acknowledging that you have to try harder (Linehan 1993a). It might mean recognizing that you are both dependent on others for help and able to handle great responsibility independently.

Understanding and adopting a dialectical thinking pattern—that two seemingly contradictory things can be true at the same time—can enable greater *cognitive flexibility*. It is often *cognitive rigidity* (that is, being stuck in thinking habitual thoughts over and over again and having the perception of limited or no alternatives) that turns normal anxiety into chronic stress.

Stretching Rigid Patterns of Thought

Marsha Linehan describes dialectical thinking as viewing reality as dynamic rather than static (Linehan 1993a). Reality is composed of opposing forces and ideas that all exist at once. This principle involves accepting multiple and sometimes contradictory truths and letting go of seeing only the extremes in situations.

ACCEPTING MULTIPLE TRUTHS

In the DBT framework, truth evolves and develops over time (Linehan 1993a). Believing that there is only one final, indisputable truth can cause conflict and anxiety and can leave you locked in a rigid pattern of thought. Of course, our world consists of facts: the earth revolves around the sun; the sun is hot. Accepting contradictory truths means acknowledging that all the facts can never be entirely known and that we each interpret the facts through our own lens of experience. My truth, seen through my lens, may be very different from yours. Neither needs to be right or wrong. Both can—and do—exist simultaneously.

LETTING GO OF EXTREME THINKING

Stress-related thoughts often seesaw between the opposite ends of a spectrum of thoughts, keeping you wildly swinging up and down in emotional intensity. With DBT, your goal is to move your thinking closer to the center of the seesaw. You can do this by moving away from extreme thinking, particularly perfectionist thinking.

BLACK VS. WHITE

Confining your views of people, actions, and events to extremes—and using words such as "good," "bad," "never," "always," "must," "should," "shouldn't," "fair," "unfair," "idiot," "stupid," and "ideal"—increases the emotional intensity of your thoughts and narrows your focus, making it more likely that you will have distorted views and exaggerated impressions. But in a dialectical worldview, you search for the gray area rather than choosing a black-and-white view of extreme thinking. You can exhibit "bad" behavior, but still be a "good" person. You can make a mistake and still be competent.

EMBRACE IMPERFECTION

Perfection is a particularly stress-inducing extreme. Do you hold the belief that if you could only achieve perfection, stress would disappear? Do you strive for the perfect home with rooms that are never messy and walls that never need painting; perfect clothes that are comfortable, fashionable, and never dirty or wrinkled; and perfect manners, performance, academics, work, and relationships?

Unfortunately a search for perfection doesn't improve our lives and it doesn't ease stress. Setting unrealistic goals with perfect standards for yourself can result in self-judgment and, ultimately, a failure to try new things in the future. Perfectionism is often accompanied by thoughts like *I'm an idiot* or *I am bad* when your attempts at absolute perfection fail. This invalidation of yourself leads to shame, hopelessness, and giving up before you have started. A need for perfection interferes with your ability to be "good enough." Having a goal of perfection keeps you focused on all the details that are not yet perfect. It keeps you from letting go and moving on. It keeps you from accepting life as it is.

• *Jen's Story*

Jen had been a successful marketing director before she left work to raise her young children. Leaving her powerful position was difficult for her, but she'd always had an image in her mind of a beautiful home filled with happy children. She told herself that to be a successful mother she must create that perfect image of home life. To achieve perfection she found herself constantly chasing after her children to pick up their messes. When her son spread his train set around the living room, she constantly worried about cleaning up while he was playing. She shouted at her four-year-old daughter when she spilled her crayons on the floor. She overscheduled her children for music, language, and multiple sports classes. She left pictures leaning against the wall for months because she couldn't find the perfect place on the wall for them and avoided having friends and family over because she worried they'd see the house when it wasn't perfect. Each day she worried about dripping faucets, sibling squabbles, dusty lamp shades, and uneaten vegetables. She believed that if she was unable to create a perfect home and a perfect childhood for her children, that meant she was a failure as a mother. Perfectionism kept her from enjoying meals that were good enough, a house that was clean enough, and children who were happy and healthy enough.

If you tend to set standards of perfection for yourself and are quite hard on yourself, begin to notice those judgmental thoughts. You can replace them with more accepting and less extreme thoughts. Jen's perfectionist thoughts are listed below, with some alternative thoughts that allow for gray areas.

Jen's Perfectionist Thoughts	Accepting, Less Extreme Thoughts
I'm a failure.	I made a mistake or it's not perfect, but it is good enough.
I'm not a good enough mother.	My children need a mother who loves them, not one who is perfect.
My children will know I'm a failure if I allow the house to get messy.	Being a role model for my children on how to handle messes and problems will help them grow into resilient adults.
I must feed my children only organic, homemade food. Anything store bought is ruining their health.	Healthy foods are best, but if we have occasional unhealthy snacks, no one will be harmed.
I must always provide a rich intellectual environment for my children. TV is destructive and erodes their intelligence.	I do puzzles, read with them, and do other stimulating activities. It's okay to watch some TV.

PRACTICE: REPLACING PERFECTIONIST THINKING

Perfectionist thinking can become a habit. To change any habit, it's essential to practice new behaviors, in this case new thoughts, over and over, until they replace the habitual behaviors.

1. Find a quiet time during the day. Take out your journal or a blank piece of paper and create a table with two columns, like the one above. Label one column "Perfectionist Thinking" and the other "Accepting, Less Extreme Thoughts."

2. Think back over the course of your day (or the previous day, if you're completing the exercise in the morning). Pay special attention to times when you felt that you failed, made a mistake, or anticipated failing or making a mistake. Remember, or if you can't remember, imagine the thoughts that you had in response to these failures and mistakes. It may help to review the thoughts that you recorded in the practice exercises in chapter 1.

3. In the Perfectionist Thinking column, write down any of your thoughts that you believe are perfectionist or extreme. You might write down a complete thought or one or two words. Words such as "failure," "ruin," "good," "bad," "never," "always," "must," "should," "shouldn't," "fair," "unfair," "idiot," "stupid," and "ideal" are signs of perfectionist thinking.

4. In the column labeled "Accepting, Less Extreme Thoughts," write alternative thoughts that are more relaxed, open, and forgiving of imperfections. To defuse extreme thoughts, replace words like "always" and "never" with milder words such as "sometimes." For thoughts that contain extreme words, such as "failure," "idiot," "impossible," or "ruin," try to look at what you achieved rather than at what you didn't.

5. If you tend to view any mistake as a failure or if you see being the best as the only definition of success, it might help to ask yourself, *How can I handle this?* or *What is positive about this problem?*

Keep this list of challenges to your perfectionist thinking. Add to it as you notice more instances of extreme thinking, and practice repeating your more accepting and moderate thoughts. Remember, it takes practice to make any life changes, even changes in your thinking.

Context and Interconnection

In Linehan's description of dialectics, we are all connected (Linehan 1993a). Our actions are also connected. Most people have dropped a pebble in the water and watched the ripples expand. Like the ripples of the pebble, our actions and the actions of others around us expand and have both intended and unintended consequences.

The challenge is to remember the influence of external circumstances when you get stuck in rigid thinking. For example, suppose during an appointment with your doctor, she is abrupt and dismissive. You conclude that she's disgusted with how you've managed your weight and doesn't think your problems are worth her time.

But it's not possible to know every influence on her or anyone else. There are many possible causes for your doctor's behavior well beyond your initial conclusion. She may be overscheduled, tired from a night of emergency calls, in need of a vacation, or frustrated with bureaucracy.

On a larger scale, the concept of interconnectedness is remembering that all interactions occur in a social world. Our actions are under our personal control, but they are also influenced and guided by our social context. Someone who has experienced violence or oppression will think and behave differently than someone who has always had access to the necessary resources for life and well-being. To adopt the view that we are all interconnected, you must look to social context when you seek to understand your actions and the actions of those around you. For example, in the case of the doctor, her work is extremely stressful, and this stress may cause her to behave dismissively. Her actions may not be about you at all.

Say Yes to Change

The final dialectical principle is that reality is continuously changing (Linehan 1993a). Change can be stressful, especially if you believe your life is changing for the worse.

According to Linehan, this principle is about accepting change, whether you believe it's positive or negative, as the essential nature of life (Linehan 1993a). Emotions become more intense and thinking more distorted if you try to stop or control change. Worries that happiness will end or that stress and anxiety will never end add to stress.

Continuous change means that a moment of happiness will pass and so will moments of anxiety. Like ocean waves, both emotions will return and leave again, flowing in and out of your life. Accepting continuous change can help you let go of the worry that positive moments will end and that negative emotions will go on indefinitely. Knowing that both the moments you love and cherish and those you find stressful and debilitating will pass allows you to be present to experience your life as it is taking place.

Observing the Content of Your Thoughts

As you read through these dialectical principles, you may wonder how they apply to your own thinking. Do extreme words, perfectionist thoughts, or a belief that you lack options seem familiar to you?

Let's look at the example of Jen. Her belief that she has to create a perfect home for her children is an extreme thought. She is operating as if this thought is fact, constantly trying to make real life match her perfect vision and considering herself a failure when, inevitably, it doesn't live up to that vision.

Jen has begun to reduce the impact of problem thinking on her stress by developing greater awareness of the content of her thoughts. Self-awareness makes it possible to distance yourself from faulty thinking and get a better perspective on the situation.

Observe Patterns in Your Thoughts

Sometimes the simple process of observing your thoughts is enough to gain objectivity and reduce the effect of your thoughts on your stress levels (Beck and Emery 2005).

However, you may also need to explore the patterns, meanings, and beliefs underlying your thoughts to lessen their stressful impact—a task that is not always easy. Aaron Beck, MD, and Gary Emery, Ph.D., propose that observing anxious and stressful thoughts is difficult for two reasons (Beck and Emery 2005):

1. When you're anxious and stressed, you're often so immersed in the emotion that it's difficult to step back and simply observe what you're thinking.

2. You might be anxious about what you will find if you look too closely.

But when you notice your thoughts without engaging in them, you create distance between yourself and what you're thinking, which decreases the power of these thoughts to activate your stress. You will notice that your thoughts will come and go. You can watch them as they pass by and make choices: engage in thinking, let the thoughts pass, or actively try to change them.

PRACTICE: EXPLORING YOUR THOUGHTS

In chapter 1 you created a stress record and completed an exercise on noticing your thoughts during stressful moments. In this exercise you'll use your notes from those exercises to begin to identify patterns in your thinking during times of stress, to identify automatic thoughts, and to uncover the meaning you attach to certain stressful thoughts. For each of these exercises, you will need to sit in a quiet place where you won't be disturbed for five to ten minutes. Bring your pen or pencil and your journal or your notes from your previous exercises.

1. Read over the thoughts that came up in the exercise Practice: Identifying Thoughts during Stress from chapter 1. If you have not completed that exercise, you can go back and do it now. If you have a lot of thoughts, you may want to choose those associated with one particular event or that occurred on one day.

2. For each thought, write down whether it focused on regrets or worries about the past, planning for the future, or anxiety and fears about the future. If you were anxious about body responses,

such as a pounding heart or shallow breathing that occurred while you were observing your thoughts, write that down as well.

3.   Label any words that were self-judgments, blame, or judgments about others. Don't edit yourself; just allow the words to come out. Often stressful thoughts become much less so when you write them down.

4.   After you've labeled your thoughts, take note of any patterns. Were you primarily planning or worried about the future? Did you ruminate about strain and conflict that occurred in past interactions with people?

5.   Now practice labeling your thoughts as they occur in your mind. For example, did you realize that you often worry about the past? For the next twenty-four hours, when you find yourself doing that, label it in your mind: *That's a worry about the past.* Don't try to change the thought, stop your thinking, or engage in the thought process. Simply labeling the patterns in your thinking will help you disengage from them and allow your thoughts to float by. Try to catch yourself engaging in the thought patterns that have become apparent to you through working in this book and simply label them as they happen.

For example, when Jen began to watch her thoughts, these were the thoughts that came up for her most often:

- *I'm such a failure.* (self-judgment focused on past actions)

- *I can't even keep the house clean.* (self-judgment focused on past)

- *Why can't I manage two children?* (worry with implied self-judgment)

- *I should be able to manage two children.* (self-judgment)

With this exercise, Jen identified that many of her stressful thoughts were self-judgments about past behaviors. Once she recognized the pattern of self-judgment and worry about past performance, she was able to label these thoughts as they occurred, which made them much less powerful.

Identify Automatic Thoughts

An *automatic thought* is an internal dialogue that occurs rapidly and repeatedly. These thoughts often occur in shorthand—just a few words or a phrase—and seem to just happen. The content of automatic thoughts often includes negative self-statements, negative beliefs, and fears about mental or physical harm. In the midst of a stressful situation, automatic thoughts can seem reasonable. For instance, Jen's automatic thoughts were *What's wrong with me? I'm losing my mind!* and *I'm going to fall apart.*

PRACTICE: IDENTIFYING AUTOMATIC THOUGHTS

1. Using your notes from the exercises in chapter 1, begin to make a list of automatic thoughts. Write down any thoughts that happen repeatedly, especially those thoughts that occur regardless of the stressor. Be sure to note those thoughts that are about harm that might come to you, because of stress (for example, losing your mind, falling apart, or going crazy).

2. As with the previous exercise, begin to label your thoughts as they occur in your mind. For this exercise, you can label any highly repetitive thought as an automatic thought. When one occurs, say to yourself, *That's an automatic thought.* If automatic thoughts happen frequently, you may find it helpful to count them. Again, don't try to change the thought, stop your thinking, or engage with the thought. Simply labeling the patterns in your thinking will help you disengage from them.

When you identify your automatic thoughts, you may recognize that although these thoughts feel quite accurate while you are in the midst of stress, they are actually exaggerated or distorted. With this realization, you may find that your anxious thoughts begin to have less power to stress you out. Identifying and labeling automatic thoughts will help you notice them and allow them to pass by without responding to them as true or factual.

Uncovering Meaning Attached to Stressful Thoughts

Meaning often comes from our beliefs and past experiences and has a significant impact on whether or not a thought is stressful. For instance, for one person the thought *I failed* could be a statement of fact. To this person, it could mean that a project, idea, or effort didn't work out. At the same time, for another person, the thought *I failed* could mean *I'm inadequate* or *I'm a disgrace*. Attaching the judgments of inadequacy and disgrace to the thought, *I failed* makes it much more likely to trigger intense emotions and a stress response.

PRACTICE: UNCOVERING MEANING

1. Read through your notes from chapter 1 again and choose one stressful thought. You might choose a thought that is a self-judgment, one that is particularly bothersome, or one that repeats often. For instance, *I'm a failure*.

2. Identify what that thought contains fear of ("X") so you can make it the subject of the following sentence: "X means (or would mean) that _____." Write down how you would fill in the blank. In the case of *I'm a failure*, you might think *Being a failure would mean that I'm incompetent* and write "I'm incompetent."

3. Now repeat step 2, only this time using the fear contained in the thought you just wrote down as "X." In other words, if you wrote "I'm incompetent," now complete the sentence "Being incompetent would mean that _____." Do this several times until you get to the heart of your worry about yourself (for example, "I'm worthless").

4. After you've identified common meanings or beliefs, begin to label your thoughts as they occur in your mind. For example, if you discovered that you connect criticism with being a failure, label those thoughts in your mind. You might choose to say to yourself, *That's a thought connected to the fear of failure.* Or you may need to create a shorter label such as "Fear of failure." As in the

previous exercises, don't try to change the thought, stop your thinking, or engage in the thought process. Simply labeling the patterns in your thinking will help create distance and reduce your reactivity to your thoughts.

Jen chose the thought *I can't even keep the house clean*. Jen's process was as follows: "Not keeping the house clean means I am imperfect as a mother. Not being perfect would mean that I'm an incompetent mother, my children are not going to be productive adults, staying home is a waste of time, and I'm wasting my children's one opportunity at childhood." She identified that she was making herself anxious by believing that messiness would cause permanent damage to her children. She began to label her thoughts as "Self-judgment" when they occurred and, with time, was able to notice them and let them pass by.

Once you have developed greater awareness of the patterns in your thinking, your automatic thoughts, and the meaning you attribute to them, you can begin to choose how to respond to these stressful thoughts as they occur. You will choose to respond to some thoughts, change others, and allow others to float by.

Evaluating and Changing Problematic Thinking

It is possible to change how you think. Many people believe that their thoughts are a part of them—an internal voice that somehow expresses who they really are. Observing your thoughts begins to give you some distance, so you can see them simply as thoughts. Whether they arise in your mind out of habit or from a belief or past experience doesn't matter. You can decide whether you want to keep a thought or whether you want to change it.

The Core of Truth in Distorted Stressful Thinking

Stress is perpetuated and intensified by worries and thoughts. When your worries and thoughts are exaggerated, rigid, or extreme, you create a distorted view of your circumstances. Nevertheless, in DBT, it is assumed that there is value in each person's point of view (Linehan 1993a). Even worries based on distorted thoughts can be understandable in context.

It is essential to remember that your stress and anxiety developed for a reason. The reality is that stressful things happen in life. Before you start to change how you're thinking, it's important to acknowledge that part of your thinking is accurate. Most exaggerated fears, stresses, and anxieties originate in something real. Past experience, traumatic events, and mood all play a role in the development of distorted thinking:

- *Past experience.* Growing up in a family that was exacting and critical or having an early experience of public humiliation can have an impact on your anxiety about speaking in groups and public settings. In another example, graduating from college during a recession and experiencing a lot of rejection in your first attempts to find a job can result in anxiety about looking for work later in life.

- *Traumatic experience.* When you have had a traumatic experience, your brain begins to react to certain trauma-related cues as if they were warning signs of danger. For example, the smell of a certain aftershave worn by an abuser or a particular hand gesture that he used may trigger a stress response. After a trauma, the activation of the stress response can happen without your conscious awareness.

- *Mood.* Your mood has a powerful effect on memory and attention. Once stressed, you are more likely to notice and attend to other stressful stimuli and to remember the stressful elements of a situation.

PRACTICE: IDENTIFYING THE ORIGINS OF DISTORTED THINKING

When you start to look at changing the thoughts that contribute to your stress and anxiety, it's important to take a moment to consider their origins.

The process of change itself can be stressful. Approaching your thoughts with understanding and compassion can help you maintain your motivation to make changes.

You will need your journal or blank paper, a pen or pencil, and five to ten quiet minutes to complete this exercise.

1. Choose one event that tends to make you anxious or stressed. It may help to refer to your notes from the exercise Practice: Identifying Times of Stress in chapter 1. You can choose an event that occurs frequently or one that is particularly stressful.

2. Think about past experiences you've had of similar events. Did your experience in your family growing up affect how you cope with this event? Is the experience somehow connected with trauma or negative consequences? Do you notice negative mood having an impact on your thinking after you've been in similar circumstances?

3. Write down a few brief sentences about why it makes sense that you have worries and anxieties about this situation. If you're not sure, try thinking of your stress as a messenger. What message has your stress been trying to communicate to you? Be open to the idea that your stressful thoughts may make sense in your current situation. Not all worries are distorted and in need of change. Some are valid responses to your current life circumstances.

4. When you notice that you are stressed about this situation in the future, practice telling yourself that it makes sense that you react the way that you do but that now it's time to respond differently. See whether validating yourself has a calming effect.

It's not giving up on wanting to change your stress response to acknowledge that there are functional, undistorted aspects of your thinking. As you read through this chapter, it is critical to keep in mind that you are not crazy for having the responses you've had and that you have been doing the best that you can (Linehan 1993a). Now it is time to learn new strategies to make changes.

Gathering Information with If-Then Predictions

If-then statements are those you make to yourself about your expectations, about how you expect events to unfold. Stress is triggered by events as they happen but also by anticipated events. Frequent anticipation of rejection, failure, or physical threat increases stress. Inaccurate if-then predictions activate the stress response in exactly the same way as accurate ones—for example, "*If* I go to the party, *then* everyone will laugh at me," "*If* I make a mistake, *then* I will be fired," and "*If* I'm not perfect, *then* I will be rejected" are all predictions that can activate a stress response.

Faulty if-then predictions can also lead you to repeatedly put yourself in situations that have negative and stressful effects. For example, "*If* I call an ex-boyfriend (who has been critical of me since the breakup), *then* he will comfort me" is a faulty, overly positive prediction that is likely to end in disappointment—a failure to get the comfort you are seeking. Both the disappointment and lack of comfort can add to your stress levels. When you frequently miscalculate the outcomes of a situation, you are likely to find yourself in negative and painful circumstances.

PRACTICE: EXPLORING IF-THEN PREDICTIONS

Instead of accepting your if-then predictions as fact, explore them.

1. Choose one situation that tends to make you anxious or stressed. You can choose the same situation as in the previous exercise, a situation that occurs frequently, or one that is particularly stressful.

2. In your journal or on a sheet of paper, complete the sentence "If X happens, then I expect (or worry) that _____ will happen," where X is the stressful event. You may need to complete and then reverse the sentence three or four times (using the same process you used earlier to attach meaning to thoughts) before you have clearly articulated your if-then prediction.

3. When you have gotten your prediction clearly articulated, rate how strongly you believe in the accuracy of your prediction on a scale

of 0–100. Zero would be totally inaccurate, and one hundred would be 100 percent accurate.

4. Over the next few days, test your prediction. For example, if your prediction is that if you make mistakes at work, you will be fired, notice when others make mistakes at work or think back to mistakes you've made in the past. Have you or your coworkers ever been fired? It's not necessary to deliberately make mistakes or create problems or harm to yourself to test your predictions. You can observe others or think back to when the event occurred in the past.

   Remember that stress and anxiety narrow your attention and focus. If you're noticing only negative outcomes, be sure to try the exercise during moments of calm to ensure that you're not filtering out positive or neutral information.

5. Now return to your earlier prediction and again rate how strongly you believe your original if-then prediction. Some of your if-then predictions may be accurate, but many may not be. Remain open to exploring these assumptions that may or may not be entirely accurate.

Remember that there is an essence of truth, even within distorted or exaggerated worries. There is something about your fear that makes sense. In a barrel of apples, there is usually one rotten apple. Faulty if-then predictions often originate in an early encounter with that rotten apple and a subsequent assumption that the rest are also bad. Don't let that one rotten apple make you think the rest are bad. Take the time now to investigate.

Changing Exaggerated or Distorted Thoughts

Becoming aware of your thinking allows you to make a choice about which thoughts are helpful and which to change.

Just telling yourself to think differently is often ineffective. If you try to simply shut down or ignore anxious thoughts, they will continue. Here are some strategies to help you shift your perspective and change your thoughts.

BECOME A NEUTRAL OBSERVER

When you're stressed, you view the world through a selective lens of intense emotion. Stress and anxiety cause you to focus on the stressful and anxiety-provoking aspects of any situation. They also make it more likely that you will remember the stressful circumstances and forget those that are not stressful.

As a result, you can end up with narrow and distorted thinking patterns when the reality may be quite different. There are two techniques you can use to widen your attention (Beck and Emery 2005):

1. Look at evidence.

2. Expand your options.

Looking at the evidence is a search for the facts and data that underlie anxious thought. When you think dialectically, you continually search for what has been left out of your understanding. You focus on the objective data that supports—or fails to support—your beliefs, expectations, and thoughts. *Intense emotion* can accompany faulty thinking, so it's helpful to imagine that you are a trusted advisor, investigating the experiences of a friend or an acquaintance. Imagining that they are someone else's thoughts, rather than your own, can get you out of the rut of seeing only the negatives.

• *Don's Story*

Don, a fifty-five-year-old father of two, was anxious that his teenage son Peter was going to make a terrible mistake and ruin his life. Don worked long hours and worried that he was not involved enough in Peter's day-to-day life. Don's anxiety was causing him to become overly critical and controlling of Peter. He had started to notice every instance in which Peter disagreed with him, disregarded rules, or challenged his authority. Recently Peter had refused to participate in a family outing on the weekend. He told his father that he needed to study but instead he watched TV all afternoon. Don immediately became anxious that Peter would never amount to anything—would become lazy, drop out of school, and never have a successful career. To better understand the evidence for his worries, Don completed a technique to be his own trusted advisor.

This technique can help you recognize automatic stressful thoughts and see events from a neutral perspective (Beck and Emery 2005).

Data	Interpretation	Observing as a Trusted Advisor
Peter missed a family outing and watched TV instead of studying. Lately Peter has not participated in a number of household events, such as helping with chores and attending family meals. Peter has maintained his A/B grades, is home by curfew, and never misses baseball practice.	*I'm failing as a father. Peter doesn't respect my authority and is going to make a terrible mistake that will ruin his life.*	*Peter is not meeting household expectations and on one occasion he watched TV instead of doing the homework he'd said he would. Nonetheless, his grades and participation in sports do not support the interpretation that he is on a road to ruining his life.*

After observing the situation as a trusted advisor, it was clear to Don that he was attributing meaning to Peter's behavior that wasn't supported by the evidence. He began to see that his assumption that Peter would make a terrible mistake was his own fear and was interfering with his ability to tolerate and respond effectively to normal teenage behavior.

PRACTICE: OBSERVING AS A TRUSTED ADVISOR

1. For this exercise you will need a quiet place where you won't be disturbed for five to ten minutes. Bring your journal or a blank piece of paper and a pen or pencil with you. Now choose a situation in which you suspect faulty thinking may be increasing your stress response.

2.   Create a table with three columns, like the one above. Label the first column "Data," the second column "Interpretation," and the third "Observing as a trusted advisor."

3.   In the "Data" column, write down the circumstances of the situation. Try to stick only to the facts. Be on the alert for words that indicate an opinion or judgment such as "fair," "should," "bad," "wrong," or "right." Try to replace these words with facts.

4.   In the "Interpretation" column, write down the meaning you make of the facts in the "Data" column. You can include your opinion, judgments, and assumptions.

5.   In the "Observing as a trusted advisor" column, imagine you are a reasonable, neutral, and truthful advisor. As this advisor, rather than as yourself, write out the meaning you might attribute to the circumstances. Remember that this advisor is meant to be neutral, so be aware of an urge to solely validate your own interpretation.

6.   Over the next few days, try repeating the "Observing as a trusted advisor" column to yourself when this situation arises or you find yourself thinking about it. It might help to write down a few short-hand comments to repeat to yourself. In Don's story, when he found himself thinking that Peter was ruining his life, he would say to himself, *Peter is not meeting all my expectations, but he is maintaining his grades and sports activities.* This thought enabled Don to respond to Peter more calmly and to respond to Peter's problem behaviors with appropriate rather than extreme consequences.

Looking at the evidence brings your thinking closer to the center of that dialectic seesaw. It helps you get out of habitual problem thoughts and consider alternative possibilities, and that level of awareness can reduce how frequently you are activating your stress response.

EXPAND YOUR OPTIONS

Dialectical thinking is about expanding your options and thinking more flexibly. To expand your options,

- remember the social context with its connections that frame any situation;

- consider other less extreme alternatives;

- accept that your truth may differ from someone else's and that both may be true; and

- be open to the inevitability of change (Linehan 1993a).

Expanding your options is about recognizing that there are thousands of contextual factors that influence behavior at any given time. Accepting opposing truths requires that you expand your thinking to include different points of view. Your own beliefs come from your past experiences. Someone else with different experiences may have a very different truth than you do. Consider Jen's story below to see how two people can interpret the same data in entirely different ways.

• *Jen's Story (continued)*

In addition to struggling with her perfectionism, Jen has always had a strained and stressful relationship with her mother. She believes that her mother wants to control her but doesn't care deeply for her. Her mother calls many times a day with criticisms and unwanted advice. She criticizes how seldom Jen visits her with the kids, the food that Jen makes for her family, the children's activities, and Jen's appearance, which her mother believes has declined since Jen left work.

Recently Jen's father began treatment for cancer, and the tension between her and her mother has increased. Jen feels constantly criticized and unable to discuss important issues with her mother. Rather than continue to view her mother's involvement in her life as rejecting and controlling, she looks at other potential options for her mother's behavior:

- *Context and interconnection.* Her mother grew up in a different time, when all meals were homemade and children played outside rather than in structured activities. Her grandparents had very exacting standards, and her mother learned the importance of maintaining certain appearances.

- *Accepting multiple truths.* Her mother wants to control her *and* her mother cares deeply for her. What Jen views as "controlling," her mother views as "guidance" and "support." Her mother's attempts to control her daughter are misguided attempts to help her. Her mother doesn't know any other way of showing care and concern.

- *Moderate, less extreme thoughts.* Her mother is not *always* controlling; she is sometimes critical and has many opinions but she can also be kind and supportive.

- *Inevitable change.* Although her mother is often critical, Jen recognizes that this intense period of criticism—rooted in her mother's stress about her father's cancer—will pass.

PRACTICE: EXPANDING YOUR OPTIONS

1. For this exercise you will need a quiet place where you won't be disturbed for five to ten minutes. Bring your journal or a blank piece of paper and a pen or pencil with you. You will again be choosing a stressful event to investigate. You can continue with an event that you've worked with in previous exercises or choose a new event that contributes to your stress levels.

2. At this point, you have had some experience describing events nonjudgmentally. First write the basic details of this event, sticking as much as you can to facts. Next, write the stressful meaning or interpretation you've made of these circumstances.

3. Now write out the four strategies to increase dialectical thinking: context and interconnection; accepting multiple truths; moderate, less extreme thoughts; and inevitable change. Use these four strategies to brainstorm alternatives to your original meaning or interpretation. You may not believe that the alternatives you generate are accurate. Still, generating alternatives helps you consider other

ways of viewing the situation and can lessen your belief that your original interpretation is the absolute truth.

Jen may never know what influences her mother's behavior, but considering other options allows her to feel cared for by her mother, decreasing the strain and stress in their relationship. When you practice more flexible thinking, you can decrease the automatic activation of the stress response.

GUIDELINES FOR TRUSTING YOUR THOUGHTS

Everyone has biases and everyone distorts reality in some way. Negative mood tends to bias you toward negative observations. It's simply how our brains work. Our brains are not computers: they have to acquire, assess, and evaluate information through a personal lens. That lens can exaggerate or minimize different aspects of your situation. At times you may exaggerate problems, ignore important information, or become rigid in your point of view.

Follow your instincts: Intuitive knowledge. *Intuitive knowledge* is different from rational thought. Intuitive knowledge is that internal sense that something just is true. It can't be proven or tested. In DBT, intuitive knowledge is described as the overlap between emotionality and intellectual thought (Linehan 1993a). Intuitive knowledge is connecting to your basic internal beliefs about yourself and the world. It is an inner understanding that you are kind or maintaining a belief that you are capable or a recognition that a given decision is the right one for you.

Know your biases and distortions. Knowing what your personal biases are and when you are most likely to fall into faulty thinking allows you to catch exaggeration, minimization, and inflexibility. When you're able to notice and correct your own distorted thoughts, you are better able to trust your thoughts as accurate reflections of the world around you.

Under acute stress, we are biased toward exaggerating the probability of negative events occurring (Warda and Bryant 1998). And, whether we're stressed or not, the information in our memory influences our predictions about the world around us, creating other biases.

If we are exposed to and remember situations that don't accurately reflect reality, then we become biased in our views. For example, if you watch the national news and see several stories in which young children are kidnapped by strangers, you may develop a faulty belief that all strangers are dangerous and that your young children are in imminent danger when they encounter anyone you don't know. The probability is that most strangers you encounter pose no danger to your children and many would likely be kind and helpful if needed. Fashion magazines provide another example of how images and information can distort your view of what is normal. The manipulated images of models and celebrities in magazines and on the Internet can distort your understanding of what ordinary women look like.

Because our memories are primarily about ourselves, we also tend to assume that our actions dominate the attention of others. As a result, we have a tendency to overestimate how others will remember our actions. For example, having made a mistake, we are likely to wonder, "What will everyone think?" Believing yourself to be in a negative spotlight, even if it's an inaccurate belief, can be uncomfortable and stressful.

Your imagination can lead to biases and distorted thoughts. Simply imagining certain outcomes can make you more likely to believe that those outcomes are possible. If you've got an active imagination or tend to visualize events in other people's lives as happening to you, this is an important bias to watch for. For example, you might hear that a friend has breast cancer. If you then imagine getting cancer yourself and picture how your family would react, the treatment, and your recovery or death, you are more likely to believe that you will get cancer. If you had not imagined yourself getting cancer, you'd be less likely to believe that you would get cancer. On the other hand, you might imagine—and as a result find yourself expecting—only extremely positive life events that never materialize, thus also causing you stress.

Your motives and expectations slant your judgments. We all favor information that confirms our beliefs. Once we've formed a judgment, we tend to ignore or gloss over inconsistent information that threatens our understanding. If you see yourself as a failure, you will forget the times you've succeeded. If you expect rejection and harsh treatment, you will gloss over the examples of others going out of their way to help you.

Even if we are not completely blind to our biases, we are usually blind to them in the present. Most people are willing to acknowledge that they have, at some time in the past, been biased in their views. However, it is much more difficult to see biases as they are currently influencing your thoughts (Gilovich, Pronin, and Ross 2004).

PRACTICE: OBSERVING BIASES

To get out of this cycle, you must observe your own thought processes and notice these automatic biases and distortions. The ability to spot your own distortions when they happen will help you develop trust in your own thinking.

1. When you're beginning to uncover your own biases, it's easiest to start by looking for them one at a time.

2. Write down possible biases in your journal or on a piece of paper. These would include exaggerating negative events, focusing on negative information, assuming you're the center of attention, imagining bad outcomes, and focusing on confirming old judgmental thinking.

3. Choose one situation that tends to stress you out. Spend a few days noticing the information and experiences that may be distorting your views. Notice the topics you see on the news or read about; situations that surround you at work, at home, and socially; topics of discussion among friends and family; and negative personal experiences (such as making a mistake). At the end of each day, write down under each possible bias situation the information or ways of thinking that could create a bias, either now or in the future.

4. On a different day, notice when you hear about other people's problems or times of crisis. As you get good at identifying when other people are telling you about their problems, notice your thoughts and imagination. Do you tend to imagine yourself in similar circumstances? At the end of the day, write down any problems or crises you encountered that you imagined would happen to you.

5. You began to uncover your expectations in the exercise Practice: Exploring If-Then Predictions. Remember that stress and anxiety narrow your attention and focus. Begin to tune in to habitual predictions of negative outcomes. Ask yourself whether you might be filtering out positive or neutral information. Write down any negative predictions that you suspect are biased.

6. After you've spent time noticing your biases, look back at your notes to see whether you can discern a pattern. Is there a type of bias that seems to have more of an impact on your thinking than others? Are there topics your thoughts seem to focus on or negative or overly positive predictions that you habitually make? Do you tend to fall into imagining dire or overly positive circumstances?

As you become proficient at identifying faulty thinking, you can choose to let those thoughts pass or to challenge them with more accurate statements.

How awful is it? De-catastrophizing. Like bias, catastrophic thoughts are a category of distorted thoughts. Are you someone who frequently expects the worst? Do you think a racing heart means a heart attack is imminent? Does a friend's divorce makes you imagine your own marriage is in danger? Does a poor economy mean you're going to lose your job?

• *Don's Story (continued)*

In addition to worrying about his son, Don was terrified of losing his job. He worked for a small start-up that was struggling in a down economy. As an executive with the company, he'd felt obligated to invest large amounts of his savings in the company. He was immobilized by anxiety about being laid off if the company went bankrupt and losing the savings he'd invested. Images of his family having to move and having to tell his children that he could no longer pay for their college education left him barely able to function at work. He imagined not only ruining his own life but also the lives of his wife and children.

Anticipating catastrophes. The problem with anticipating potential catastrophe is that in our anticipation, we tend to imagine every possible dire consequence (Beck and Emery 2005). In Don's case, as in most cases, what he imagined might happen was consistently worse than the likely reality. Don had worked in start-ups for much of his career, and this was not the first time he'd been faced with being laid off. During a downturn in the economy, fifteen years prior, he'd been laid off and was then out of work for nine months. His wife had returned to work part-time, and the kids had switched from private to public schools. There was a significant disruption, but it had not ruined the family's life. Don's images of catastrophe failed to take into account the resilience and strength of his wife and children and the fact that the family could survive and be happy in different financial circumstances. He also discounted the real possibility that friends and colleagues would help him find work, as they had in the past.

PRACTICE: CHALLENGING CATASTROPHIC THOUGHTS

Sometimes it feels as if catastrophe is around every corner. The fear and stress you experience when anticipating an impending crisis can be debilitating and can keep you from living your life right now.

1. For this exercise you will need five to ten quiet minutes, your journal or a blank piece of paper, and a pen or pencil. You will again be choosing a stressful event to investigate. Look for a situation in which you expect disaster, find yourself asking "What if" questions (such as "What if I got cancer?" or "What if I lost my job?"), or are ruminating on a small event (such as misremembering someone's name in a social situation) and overemphasizing its importance.

2. In your journal or on a piece of paper, answer the following questions: What do I imagine will happen? How might my imagination be worse than reality? What are the positive aspects of the situation that I might be overlooking (including support from friends or family, areas of my life that are not in crisis, connecting with others over making mistakes, and being human)?

3. Now write out a challenge to your catastrophic thought or image. You can look back to the dialectical principles of thought to develop a challenge. For instance, you might want to think *Change is inevitable* or you might want to tone down extreme thoughts and change such a thought as *I can't handle it* or *It's a disaster* to *The situation is difficult, but I will manage* or *I'm disappointed by the situation*. Over

the next few days, pay attention to your thoughts and notice times when you begin to think about this situation. At those times, focus on your breathing to calm yourself and repeat your challenge to yourself. Don's was *This situation is a challenge for the whole family, but we will meet it together.*

The reality is that painful life events do happen. This book is not about pretending that life is not difficult at times. It is about helping you survive difficult times without excessive worry and suffering.

Wrap-Up

The goal of this chapter was to investigate your thoughts and learn how to effectively respond to them, change them, or let them pass by. This chapter explored how faulty, rigid, or distorted thinking can activate and exacerbate stress. I introduced you to the concept of dialectical thinking, with its focus on cognitive flexibility, along with exercises to help you observe the content of your thoughts, begin to identify predictions that impact your levels of stress, and change problematic thinking. By completing the practice exercises, you applied principles of dialectical thinking such as letting go of extreme thinking, accepting multiple truths, seeing contextual interconnections, and recognizing a constant state of change.

These strategies increase the flexibility of your thoughts; provide alternatives to habitual, stuck thinking patterns; and allow you to accept contradictory points of view. Because your thoughts and beliefs about the events in your life determine whether you interpret an event as threatening, and therefore stressful, this process of expanding your thinking is key to releasing you from unnecessary stress.

CHAPTER 3

Using Acceptance Strategies

We don't have complete control over our environment, our health, or the people around us, so we are all sure to experience stressful life events. These are those moments when we're faced with illness, death, deadlines, competition on the job, financial challenges, or changes in our family. They happen when any changes, positive or negative, occur in our lives, such as when we have a baby, fail to achieve or meet our expectations, or have an accident.

Some people seem to endure change and become stronger, while others are knocked off balance and find themselves escaping into negative and unhealthy behaviors, such as self-injury, overspending, or drinking. The skills in this chapter are designed to be short-term strategies for surviving the upheaval caused by stressful life events. These are essential life skills that help us carry on, whether we've lost our sense of security, are faced with problems that we can't immediately solve, or are overwhelmed by the demands of a promotion at work.

Getting through major life changes when you're experiencing stress and anxiety requires two types of strategies:

1. Accepting life in the moment

2. Tolerating and surviving the emotions that accompany the change

This chapter focuses on the first type—acceptance strategies designed to improve your ability to accept yourself and the current situation nonjudgmentally. Chapter 4 focuses on the second type—strategies to tolerate and survive the emotions that accompany stressful life events.

The assumption behind the acceptance skills is that pain, stress, and change are a part of life and that avoiding and denying this fact leads to increased suffering or stress. Strategies for coping with the emotions that accompany major life changes focus on finding ways to tolerate these emotions without avoidance and without behaving in ways that create additional problems or make the situation more overwhelming.

When Life Veers Offtrack: Accepting and Tolerating Life Events

According to Linehan (1993b), simply refusing to accept and tolerate a situation does not magically make it change to suit our needs and desires. We resist accepting situations because it means acknowledging that we have not gotten what we want or that our life has changed and that we are faced with a situation that is uncertain and scary. However, acknowledging, enduring, and accepting painful situations or great change decreases rather than increases the stress we suffer.

Stressful situations happen to everyone. It's impossible to go through life without experiencing a loss or death, being rejected, failing, having an accident, being physically harmed, feeling threatened, or experiencing an unexpected gain. We hope that these stressful situations don't happen often, but the reality is that they happen to all of us. They appear in different forms in each of our lives, but whether we are Oprah Winfrey or John Doe, we cannot eliminate stressful events from our lives.

Responding to Life Events

The following list was adapted with permission from a study done by Thomas Holmes and Richard Rahe (Holmes and Rahe 1967). The researchers found these to be the events that contribute most to life stress. Look over the list to determine whether you have recently experienced any of these stressful life events. Simply acknowledging stressful circumstances can help you begin to improve how you cope.

- Spouse's death
- Divorce
- Marriage separation
- Jail term
- Death of a close relative
- Injury or illness
- Marriage
- Fired from job
- Marriage reconciliation
- Retirement
- Major change in the health of a loved one
- Pregnancy
- Sexual difficulties

- Birth, adoption, parent moving in
- Business adjustment
- Major change in finances—for better or worse
- Death of a close friend
- Changing career path or line of work
- Major change in arguments with spouse—increase or decrease
- Taking on a mortgage
- Foreclosure
- Promotion or demotion
- Child leaving home—college, marriage, military service
- In-law troubles
- Outstanding personal achievement

For different people the same type of event— say, a divorce—may cause dramatically different amounts of stress based on individual circumstances. However, regardless of the specific circumstances, when any one of these events occurs in your life, the tension, uncertainty, changes to routine, and upheaval are typically central to your experience of stress.

Some things happen suddenly and cause abrupt change. We're heading in one direction and we find ourselves unexpectedly out of a job, injured in a car accident, or having lost someone important. Other changes, like retirement or a new baby, can be planned and expected. However, the changes that accompany even positive and planned life events can cause considerable stress and anxiety.

What we do when these circumstances arise makes a significant difference in how long we experience the stress and anxiety they trigger. When we're afraid of the change that a life event represents, it is common to respond by rejecting the event. This rejection happens in both our thoughts and our behaviors. How many times have you responded to life changes by doing these things?

- Struggling to fix an unfixable problem

- Avoiding thinking about the situation and anything related to it

- Refusing to make necessary changes

- Reacting from anger and fear and making the situation worse

Acceptance, on the other hand, reduces the additional stress and anxiety generated by avoiding and reacting to the situation with extreme emotion. If you are in circumstances that you don't like, acceptance allows you to focus energy on solving the problems the situation presents. Acceptance allows you to do what works in the situation rather than make it worse.

• *Kate's Story*

Kate's son has behavioral issues. At first he seemed simply to be a difficult child. He didn't sleep through the night, threw tantrums at meal times, and was unable to focus and play quietly on his own. He is Kate's oldest child, and Kate, who is a successful businesswoman, can see only his willfulness and defiance. As he's grown older, his problems have also grown. He's required to be in special classes at school because he's unable to follow class routines. He's aggressive around other children: on one occasion, he threw crayons at other children and yelled obscenities at the rest of the class. His behavior is so out of control at home that Kate has tried blocking the door with furniture to keep him in a time-out and constantly has to intervene to stop him from hitting and taunting his younger brothers.

Kate is under constant stress and describes his behavior as "ruining the family." She continues to view her son as demanding and refuses any suggestion that he may have mental health issues. She avoids books about the topic and rejects suggestions that she seek help. Her husband would like to seek help for their son, and their disagreement on this issue has led to conflict in their marriage. Kate desperately wants her son to be "normal" and she refuses to see his behavior as a result of anything other than disobedience.

Hanging on to Expectations

Social psychology research shows that our motives and expectations slant our view of reality (Greenberg, Pyszczynski, and Solomon 1982). When people are faced with life events that require them to give up long-held expectations, they tend to ignore or gloss over inconsistent information that threatens the way they understand their reality.

Take the example of Kate. Accepting that her son has a disability would require her to give up her current expectations for his future. Instead, she hangs on to the belief that he has complete control over his behavior and is simply disobedient. She glosses over his more extreme behaviors and refuses to hear any potential causes for his behavior that differ from her own point of view. She is attempting to control reality with the strength of her will.

Having a will of steel and staying the course despite obstacles can be a great asset in achieving goals. Many people find success through persistence and hard work. But willing reality to change and persisting in doing so despite our true circumstances merely creates additional stress and suffering and keeps us spinning our wheels.

To move forward, we must first learn to acknowledge and tolerate that we have been handed a life-changing event. When we accept the situation in which we find ourselves, we are no longer trapped by our own struggle to fix or change it. We are not stuck in denial or on insisting that we get what we want. We are no longer caught up in a need for control. Continually struggling to avoid what has already happened takes time and tremendous energy. That time and energy could be better spent on dealing with things as they are now and creating a life that incorporates this new reality.

Getting to Acceptance

According to Linehan (1993b), acceptance involves engaging in specific activities that decrease the body's stress response as well as employing thought processes that help us understand and accept life-changing events. The activities that follow focus on how to get your body into a more calm and relaxed state, which will have a calming effect on your emotions and thoughts. The thought processes described are designed to help you let go of your fight with reality and to choose to accept and respond to the situation as it is, not as you want it to be.

Getting Your Body into a More Accepting State

Our bodies and our minds work together. It's impossible to completely separate the two. If we're worried about something, our bodies will respond to our worry thoughts. Everyone experiences stress differently, but stress and worry often cause our bodies to become tense, nervous, jittery, or breathless.

On the other hand, if our bodies are jittery— say, from too much coffee—our minds will respond to that jumpy feeling and will interpret it as stress or anxiety. In this case, our minds have responded to a physical state.

It's hard to focus on identifying, acknowledging, and accepting what we cannot change in life if we're physically highly activated from an acute stress response. The physical response to stress can include urges to cry or scream. You may notice your own irritability or quick temper. The urge to escape from the pressures of crisis and stressful life events can be hard to ignore. If you don't have strategies to manage your stress, you can end up escaping into risky and problematic behaviors.

In the example above, Kate is terrified of facing the possibility that her son has problems beyond normal disobedience. She lives her life in a frenzy and a constant state of stress. Whether she's working, dealing with school problems, or managing the kids in the house, she's always revved up and always avoiding looking at her son's difficulties from a different perspective.

There are many relaxation techniques designed to calm the body. If you have one that works for you, you can use that. The techniques that I describe here are specifically effective in getting your body into a more accepting attitude.

FOCUS ON BREATHING

Thich Nhat Hanh, in his book *Peace Is Every Step: The Path of Mindfulness in Everyday Life,* wrote, "While we practice conscious breathing, our thinking will slow down, and we can give ourselves a real rest. Most of the time, we think too much, and mindful breathing helps us to be calm, relaxed and peaceful" (1991, 11).

A focus on breathing is an important part of treatment for stress, panic, and anxiety. The advantage of using breathing to calm the body is that we are breathing all the time, whether or not we're paying attention to it, so it's easy and natural to focus on the breath. It's also possible to focus on our breathing anywhere and anytime—such as in the middle of a meeting at work, when we're on the phone, or when we're stuck in traffic—without calling attention to ourselves,.

Focusing on breathing has many benefits:

- It is a natural and effective tool to prevent scattered or fractured thinking.

- It is a way to connect your body to your thoughts.

- When your mind becomes scattered, it is a way to refocus.

- Focusing on breathing generally has a calming effect.

- It can help to anchor you in the present moment.

In each exercise, focus on bringing your awareness to your breathing. Your mind may wander from your breathing, or you may have judgments about your ability to stay focused. It is normal to feel that way. If you do feel awkward, just notice that feeling and let it pass. If you get fidgety, just notice the urge to fidget and let it pass. If you lose focus or find you are distracted by sounds, gently bring your mind back to your breath and begin the exercise again. Allow yourself to try these exercises without analyzing, judging, or doubting yourself.

PRACTICE: BREATHING EXERCISES

Follow these steps for each of the exercises below:

1. Read through the instructions.

2. Practice, this first time, in a quiet place where you're unlikely to be disturbed.

3. Allow yourself three to five minutes to practice.

4. Remember that distractions and loss of focus are normal. Bring yourself back to the exercise if you notice you're offtrack.

5. Incorporate your practice into more stressful experiences as you become more proficient in the exercises.

Counting your breaths. With each of these exercises, you will begin by tuning in to the feeling of your breath coming in and out of your body. Focus on breathing and knowing that you're breathing.

1. Get settled in a comfortable position.

2. Focus attention on your breath.

3. Inhale, filling your lungs.

4. Exhale and with each exhale, count: 1 for the first exhale, 2 for the second exhale, and so on until you reach 10.

5. When you reach 10, start over at 1. Should you lose count at any time, start over at 1.

Fill/empty breath. One of the simplest exercises is to focus on your breath entering and leaving your body. It's easy to remember and can change your focus when you're stuck in worry.

1. Get settled in a comfortable position.

2. Focus attention on your breath.

3. Inhale, filling your lungs.

4. Say "fill" to yourself as you inhale.

5. Say "empty" to yourself as you exhale.

6. If you are distracted, gently bring your mind back to your breath and say "fill" on the inhale and "empty" on the exhale.

Balloon breath. This exercise helps when your mind is racing, ruminating, or caught up in worry. It takes your full attention and requires you to slow your breathing, which can derail your persistent and intrusive thoughts.

1. Imagine your lungs are a balloon. Slowly inhale and as you do, imagine that your lungs are filling, like a balloon. Try to fill the balloon completely.

2. Now exhale slowly. Keep the image of the balloon in mind and try to push all the air out. After a few breaths, try to extend the exhalation. This will allow you to empty your lungs of more air.

3. Continue the balloon breath for ten to twenty breaths. If you start feeling tired or dizzy while practicing, stop and return to normal breathing. You can practice this exercise while walking, sitting, or standing.

The first few times you do breathing exercises can feel awkward. Keep practicing and it will become more natural.

Following your breath while slowing your pace. Deliberately slowing the pace of your actions will help you to reduce tension in your body and slow your racing thoughts.

1. Choose any activity that you typically do quickly and without much thought. For instance, you might choose checking e-mail, mopping the kitchen floor, making a cup of coffee, or having a conversation.

2. Notice the flow of your breath and then deliberately slow the speed of your actions while you are engaged in that activity. Move

your body 50–75 percent slower than you normally would. You don't need to match your breathing to your movements. Just continue to notice your breathing as you move slowly and deliberately.

3. Follow your breath while remaining aware of the details of your movement. Don't try to hurry.

4. If you find yourself getting lost in what you're doing, refocus on your breath.

Wave breathing. Our breathing throughout the day and night can take many forms. It can be shallow and fast, slow and deep, irregular or rhythmic. The one thing that is consistent is that, like waves in an ocean, our breath comes in and goes out. Over and over—changing in quality, tempo, and strength—but consistently in and out. This exercise is about awareness of breath, not altering the breath.

1. Center your attention on your breath and notice it coming in and out.

2. Notice whether it is crashing in and out like waves in a high storm or gently rising and falling like a calm sea.

3. Find the rhythm of your breath and keep your attention focused there.

4. If you are distracted, gently bring your mind back to the continual rise and fall of your breathing.

Using breathing exercises to focus attention and slow your body's stress response takes practice. The first few times can be frustrating and full of distractions. Try to practice at least one breathing exercise a day for the next week. The more you incorporate these exercises into your daily life, the more effective they will be for you.

FOCUS ON THE BODY

Intense stress, triggered by unexpected or overwhelming circumstances, is accompanied by intense physical sensations. If you're experiencing stress and anxiety, your body is also experiencing stress and anxiety. Sweating, jumpiness, having a lump in your throat, feeling breathless, muscle tension, feeling a heaviness in your stomach, and getting cold are all physical sensations associated with stress and anxiety.

PRACTICE: EXERCISES TO CALM THE BODY

As with the breathing exercises, follow these steps for each of the exercises below:

1. Read through the instructions.

2. Practice, this first time, in a quiet place where you're unlikely to be disturbed.

3. Allow yourself three to five minutes to practice.

4. Remember that distractions and loss of focus are normal. Bring yourself back to the exercise if you notice you're offtrack.

5. Incorporate your practice into more stressful experiences as you become more proficient in the exercises.

Walking with a mantra. Often your day is broken up by moments when you are walking. When you're under stress, the time spent walking from the car to the office, heading through the aisles of the grocery store, or walking on a track for exercise is often filled with worry and anxious rumination or mindless drifting between thoughts without focused concentration. This exercise will help you use walking to develop your ability to focus your attention and concentration.

1. First choose a mantra or word to repeat as you walk. You will want to choose something simple that can be repeated with each step. Some suggestions include a mantra focused on the physical act of walking such as "Heel, toe, heel, toe" or simply the word "walk" or "step." You could also choose a mantra focused on a state of mind, for example, "calm" or "slow." You might want to put a few words together, for instance, "Walking calmly" or "With each step, I slow my mind."

2. Find a place to walk where you have a few uninterrupted moments. You can be inside or out, on a crowded street or by yourself, so long as you won't be disturbed.

3. Begin by walking and noticing the physical experience of walking. Notice the feel of your body as you walk; for example, you might focus on your foot as it touches the ground beneath you, the muscles of your legs as you take a step, or the swing of your arms. Once you feel centered in your walking, use your mantra or word with your steps. Say one or two words with each step. If you become distracted, refocus on the physical act of walking and on repeating your mantra. Continue walking this way for three to five minutes or until you feel calmer.

The first few times you do walking mindfulness can feel awkward or uncomfortable. Don't let that stop you; just notice those awkward feelings and return to your walking and mantra.

Air. A simple meditation in which you tune in to physical sensations can be used to reduce tension and improve the connection between mind and body. This is an exercise that you can use at any time, whether you're standing in line at the bank or sitting at your desk at work.

To reduce built-up tension and stress, this exercise asks you to notice the air around your body.

1. Begin by bringing your attention to your breath. Inhale and exhale a few times. As you breathe, draw your attention to the air surrounding your body. Notice the air as it touches your body. Is it still and unmoving or is there a breeze or movement in the air? If it's still, notice that sense of stillness against your skin.

2. Continue to breathe and bring your attention to the temperature of the air surrounding your body. Is it comfortable? Is it cool or warm?

3. Focus on the areas of your body, one at a time. Breathe and notice the physical sensation of air on your hands, arms, and face. Notice areas that you normally don't focus on, such as the space around your toes, the back of your neck, your ankles, or the inside of your elbows. Notice both exposed areas and those parts of your body covered with clothing. How do those areas feel the air differently?

4. After you've gone through each area of the body, simply rest, noticing the physical sensation of air surrounding you. If you are in a quiet place and undisturbed, allow yourself three to five minutes to breathe and feel the air on your body. Let each breath increase your sense of calm.

This exercise is not for everyone, but many find it helpful in letting go of tension and disconnecting from daily worries.

A relaxed smile. Smiling improves mood and reduces tension. It often seems like a forced smile only increases tension and irritation, but relaxed smiling enhances positive mood for two reasons: (1) people react more positively to you when you look happy and (2) "facial feedback" fools your brain into thinking you are happy (Kleinke, Peterson, and Rutledge 1998). In DBT a half-smile is used to help you accept reality (Linehan 1993b).

1. Begin by relaxing. Let go of the tension in your face, neck, and shoulder muscles and turn up the corners of your lips slightly. A tense smile is a grin. A relaxed smile is one with slightly upturned lips and loose facial muscles. Try to adopt a serene facial expression. Either pick a spot in the room to focus your eyes on or close your eyes. Breathe and smile.

2. Continue the practice for two to three minutes or until you feel calmer.

With each of these exercises, it's common to lose focus. The more you practice them, the less your mind will wander. Try not to judge your practice as a success or a failure. After you have tried each of the exercises, note which were the most calming for you. Over time and with practice, the other exercises may work just as well, but initially, the exercises that were most calming are the ones to try when your stress levels are high.

Principles for Accepting Life-Changing Events

Once you have slowed your body's responses to stress, your mind is in a better place to make a choice to accept the situation or circumstances that are causing you stress and anxiety.

RADICAL ACCEPTANCE

Some think that acceptance is a state that simply comes with time, patience, or understanding. This misconception can lead to passivity and feeling out of control of your own state of mind. The truth is that acceptance is active, not passive, and it requires a choice. *Radical acceptance*, a DBT skill, involves facing reality rather than rejecting and judging it (Linehan 1993b). You must commit to accepting the current circumstances over and over in diverse situations. Each time your mind tells you it's unfair or shouldn't be as it is, you remind yourself to accept it.

In Kate's story, choosing to accept the situation involves acknowledging that her son has behavioral problems beyond disobedience. She will need to admit that she doesn't know what might help her son and be open to exploring alternative causes for his problem behaviors.

PRACTICE: BENEFITS AND COSTS OF RADICAL ACCEPTANCE

It is helpful to first think through the benefits and costs of changing your outlook before making a choice to accept a situation.

Benefits of radical acceptance. This exercise helps you explore the benefits of changing your point of view. Think of a situation that is stressful, one that you have trouble accepting. You might be having difficulty acknowledging that the work environment has changed and there is no longer a market for your skills, or you might be procrastinating and avoiding school assignments because you feel terrified of being judged harshly by your professors.

1. Find a quiet time during the day, take out your journal or a blank piece of paper, and complete the sentence "The benefits of accepting _____." In the blank space, write out the life event you are avoiding thinking about or wishing were not occurring.

2. Below the sentence, write a list of potential benefits of accepting rather than fighting the situation that is causing you stress. It might be helpful to think about long-term as well as short-term changes that would occur with acceptance. If you're having

trouble, you may want to think about the benefits of acknowledging or tolerating the problem rather than fighting or denying it.

When Kate explored the benefits of accepting her son's difficulties, she saw that acceptance would allow her to explore opportunities to get him help and support, which might significantly improve his ability to function at school and in social situations.

Costs of accepting stressful life events. Acceptance also comes with a cost. When we fight, avoid, procrastinate, or try to fix something that we have no control over, we do so for good reason, usually because we're getting something out of trying to make sure things stay the same. It's important not to ignore the cost of acceptance when making a choice to accept. For this exercise, you'll explore the costs of accepting your situation.

1. Find a quiet time during the day and take out your journal or a blank piece of paper. Complete the sentence "The costs of accepting _____." In the blank space, write out the life event you are avoiding thinking about or wishing were not occurring.

2. Below the sentence, write a list of potential costs of accepting rather than fighting the situation that is causing you stress. Again, it might be helpful to think about long-term as well as short-term changes that would occur with acceptance. Remember that we avoid painful situations for a reason. What are you getting out of your nonacceptance?

In Kate's story, the intense fear and anxiety of acknowledging her son's problems kept her from actively dealing with them. She didn't want to give up on all the dreams and expectations she'd had for how his life would be, nor did she want to face her fears that he might never function well at school or in social situations.

Review your analysis. Examining forces that have an impact on how you view your current situation can help you make an active choice to acknowledge difficult life circumstances.

1. Now take a moment to review the benefits and costs of acknowledging your stressful situation.

2. List the long-term benefits from the first list and compare them to the short-term costs from the second list. Are short-term emotional costs keeping you from important long-term benefits?

Kate realized that her son had a better chance of getting the help he needed and improving his long-term social and emotional functioning if she accepted his situation. She also realized that her refusal to change how she responded to her son's problems was affecting her home life and her work performance. Although it was painful, she decided that experiencing fear and anxiety in the short term was worth the longer-term benefits to her son and in her own life.

When the world seems unfair and you're feeling stuck, anxious, or frantic, it's natural to want to give up, try to fix what can't be fixed, or simply refuse to tolerate the situation. It's difficult to focus on doing what works instead of trying to impose your will on reality. Emotion can interfere with your ability to know what is needed in each situation. Taking the time to think through the benefits and costs of acceptance can help you simply do your best, whatever the world throws at you.

USING METAPHOR TO GET TO ACCEPTANCE

In a 2008 study, McMullen and colleagues found that participants who used metaphors to understand acceptance were better able to tolerate painful tasks. Metaphors are pervasive in everyday life. We often use them to describe an experience, as when we're explaining to a friend that a panic attack feels like being trapped in an airless room and having to struggle to breathe. Metaphors give us immediately recognizable images that enable us to understand abstract concepts, like acceptance.

To shift your automatic thought patterns away from fighting, avoiding, or refusing to make changes, review the metaphors in the table below and identify those that appeal to you. When you're struggling to accept a situation that you don't want to accept, repeat the metaphor to yourself. For instance, you might say to yourself *There I go again, trying to row upstream in a canoe without a paddle.*

Below are some common ways people deny or avoid problems and some metaphors that might be helpful in moving them into a more accepting mind-set.

Examples of fighting, denial, and avoidance	Acceptance metaphors
• Fighting inevitable changes • Being stuck in rigid thinking about the situation	You are • *trying to go upstream in a canoe without a paddle;* • *asking the wind to stop blowing;* • *trying to stop the leaves from falling.* Acceptance is • *floating with the current;* • *feeling the wind on your face;* • *watching the leaves fall.*
• Refusing to make necessary changes • Avoiding problems	You are • *a boat drifting at sea or refusing to steer toward the port.* Acceptance is to • *sail rather than drift aimlessly.*
• Struggling to fix an unfixable problem • Trying to change what can't be changed	You are • *repairing the roof in the middle of a tornado.* Acceptance is • *keeping safe and ensuring the safety of others in a storm shelter.*

PRACTICE: DEVELOPING A PERSONAL ACCEPTANCE METAPHOR

The discovery of a metaphor that fits you, personally, and underscores a particular experience helps to make that experience understandable within the context of your life. Personal metaphors make your past and present as well as your hopes and dreams coherent. Self-understanding can begin with a personal metaphor that makes sense of your life and the meaning of your experience.

1. Develop an awareness of metaphors in your life. They come to us from literature, movies, music, history, and our personal experience.

2. Notice any of your past or present experiences that can form the basis of a metaphor. What are some ways that your personal expertise can lend itself to a metaphor? For instance, as a therapist, one of my personal metaphors might be "Acceptance is like being present with a client even when she's in pain rather than trying to convince her that she is happy." Some other examples: "Acceptance is like playing cards: you have to play with the hand you're dealt," "If you swim against a strong current, you end up going backward," and "When sailing, you must work with the wind to get where you want to go."

3. When you notice or hear a metaphor, try it on. Look at life through the lens of the metaphor and see whether it helps to bring focus.

4. If you're in the midst of a painful or difficult life event, try on some of the metaphors above. Do any of them help you change your thinking about your circumstances? Are you better able to tolerate the situation?

It's important to continually develop metaphors that are meaningful to you in your life. They can be tremendously helpful when you find yourself fighting your nature or the circumstances in which you find yourself.

MAKING ACCEPTANCE A HABIT

Choosing to accept is a process that happens internally. You must identify those moments when you are beginning to fight, give up, or avoid and then make the choice to accept.

PRACTICE: MAKING ACCEPTANCE A HABIT

Although it's difficult, you can make accepting reality a habit. If done regularly, acceptance can reduce stress and anxiety and improve your ability to identify and solve the problems in your life.

1. Over the next two to three days, pay attention to times when you are fighting, avoiding, or stubbornly refusing to accept a situation.

2. Regularly practice the body acceptance exercises from earlier in this chapter to slow down your body and mind's response to stress. As you practice these body awareness exercises, allow thoughts of what you're trying to accept to enter your mind.

3. Make a choice to accept the situation.

    a. If necessary, call to mind the cost/benefit analysis you've done.

    b. Focus on an acceptance metaphor.

    c. Imagine yourself accepting the situation.

4. Repeat these steps as you come up against situations you have trouble accepting until you begin to automatically accept situations rather than automatically fight them.

Wrap-Up

This chapter focused on acknowledging, tolerating, and accepting painful and distressing life events. Even positive life changes can be overwhelming and stressful. It can be difficult to face change, threatening circumstances, and feared events. But avoidance, refusal to change, or attempts to make the situation turn out as you wish only add to your pain and suffering. This chapter described strategies to quiet and relax the body that also have a calming effect on your thinking and principles and strategies to help you face reality, including radical acceptance and making acceptance a habit.

CHAPTER 4

Using Crisis-Survival Strategies

Accepting that events have disrupted your life reduces the pressure and anxiety of fighting change. Acceptance can ease the impact of overwhelming positive change as well as upsetting life circumstances. However it often takes concrete, practical strategies to tolerate acute and prolonged stress without resorting to tactics that are risky, will make change more difficult, or will make your problems worse. When you're overwhelmed by the strain of difficult life events—when you feel on edge or like you're losing control—you must have strategies for doing what works to get you through the moment of crisis.

Life-Event Survival Skills

The strategies in this chapter are designed to reduce contact with things that upset you, help you comfort and nurture yourself, and improve how you are thinking about the crisis. Linehan developed these essential and straightforward strategies to help you get through adversity without making your situation worse (Linehan 1993b). The strategies include getting mental and physical distance from problems, self-soothing, and finding ways to improve how your body and mind are responding to the event.

• Carl's Story

Carl, a thirty-seven-year-old father of two, had just started in a new and challenging position at work. He'd been promoted to this position, which required significantly longer hours and more travel, right after his wife left full-time work following the birth of their second child. The new baby was difficult and didn't sleep well, and Carl felt stressed by the pressure of his new role as sole provider for the family. He was anxious to prove that he could handle the new role at work, take care of the family finances, and, at the same time, provide support to his wife, who was exhausted and stressed by sleepless nights and caring for a toddler and a colicky baby. It was at this time that Carl's younger brother was diagnosed with leukemia and designated Carl to make decisions about his health care. Carl was overwhelmed with worry for his brother, pressure to perform at work, guilt that he was not providing support to his wife, and demands to make decisions about his brother's finances and medical treatment. He suddenly found himself making a two-hour daily commute to oversee his brother's treatment, conflicting with his family around specifics of his brother's care, overwhelmed with sadness and grief at unexpected moments, and taking business calls at the hospital and on the road. Every moment seemed beset with anxiety and tension. He questioned every decision he made and felt he was unable to meet all of his responsibilities. Carl wanted to escape from all the stress and pressure in his life.

Getting Distance

When you suppress and avoid all contact with emotional pain, you cut yourself off from the possibility of coping and moving past the pain. Avoidance guarantees that the pain will continue. However, there are also times when it is healthy to distract yourself from pain and stress. Life events and the uncertainty they cause cannot always be immediately processed. Some situations call for us to be able to function despite the turmoil we are currently experiencing. It is at these times that strategies to distance yourself from the event are essential. In the short term, they are effective in getting you through those difficult moments. They can help you return to work or school and survive day-to-day life despite external stressors.

To function in the midst of instability, you must find ways to give yourself a mental break from the pressure, worry, and rumination that often accompany stress. Getting mental distance will allow you to work, carry out normal day-to-day functions, and concentrate for at least short periods of time—all of which are key to surviving the change without other aspects of your life spiraling out of control and causing you more problems.

To get a break from your worry, you must

- identify activities that distract you and consume your attention, even briefly;

- engage in those activities with some regularity.

What each person finds distracting and absorbing is an individual matter. You may need to remember and engage in activities that have worked in the past or try out new methods. Having an outlet, any outlet, for stress-related frustration decreases the physiological stress response. Distraction, particularly with something that is positive for you, is a central feature of a frustration-reducing outlet for stress. It's important to generate a long list of potential activities so that if one stops working, you can try out another. The *Distract Assessment* is based on components of a DBT skills-training strategy and is designed to generate a list of activities that can create temporary distance from stressful thoughts and events (Linehan 1993b).

PRACTICE: DISTRACT ASSESSMENT

Find a quiet time during the day and take out your journal or a blank piece of paper to answer the questions below. Brainstorm a list for each of the questions in the assessment. Quantity breeds quality, so don't censor yourself. The goal is to generate a list of twenty to thirty activities, both large and small, that you can do at different times to take you away from your stress and anxiety, even if it's for brief moments. Aim to generate a minimum of five possibilities for each number in the assessment.

1. *What types of activity do you find absorbing?* Are you a sports nut? Do you love to read or garden? Did you grow up playing tennis? Or do you love to cook? Most people don't love to clean, but many find it distracting. Mowing the lawn, washing the car, and woodworking are all the kinds of activities in which you can immerse yourself. Here are some other activities to consider: reading a book or magazine, painting your nails, curling your hair, arranging outfits

in your closet, doing laundry or ironing, drawing, painting, scrapbooking, taking photos, doing yard work, sewing, knitting, cooking or baking, building models, singing along with music, going for a walk or hike, playing an instrument, calling a friend, writing a letter or e-mail, or exercising.

2. *What draws you out of your own problems?* Sometimes helping others provides relief from our own stress. You may think of personal ways to give to others, such as helping a child with homework, unexpectedly vacuuming the house, or asking a friend about his or her concerns. You may also think of giving to the community or world by volunteering, going to a pet shelter and walking the dogs, recycling, or doing a charity walk for a favorite cause.

3. *What can you do that leaves you feeling neutral or the opposite of stressed-out?* Are there activities that trigger emotions that are inconsistent with stress, such as happiness, joy, or contentment? To find these types of activities, ask yourself what you like to do in your leisure time. Do you watch funny movies, follow a TV series, solve sudoku, play cards, or do crossword puzzles? Does '80s music make you want to dance? Does the quiet of a museum also quiet your mind? Think of activities, such as solving puzzles, that require mental concentration and keep your mind too busy for distressing thoughts. Also consider activities that generate emotions other than stress, such as watching a romantic comedy.

4. *What can you do to give yourself a small physical jolt?* Sometimes when we're stuck in our thoughts, we need a physical shake to get off the stress track and onto a new one. These sorts of physical jolts could come from such things as spicing your burgers with hot chili peppers, jumping in a cold pool, rubbing ice on your neck and wrists, or taking a hot (but not too hot) shower. They also come from physical activities and sports that are exciting and exhilarating, such as waterskiing, trapeze lessons, riding a roller coaster, and simulating skydiving in a wind tunnel.

5. *Can you compare yourself to people who are worse off than you? It may sound odd, but when you're under stress and feeling like you can barely handle life right now, it can be helpful to compare yourself to people who are obviously*

worse off than you. Thinking about orphans in Haiti or civilian life in Afghanistan can help put your own problems in perspective. Thinking about living in a place where life expectancy is less than fifty years and average annual income is $500 can put your own health, income, and financial troubles into perspective. Remembering that some people are homeless and without families can change your outlook on your own living situation. Even comparing yourself to those immediately around you—for example, a sister who has asthma or a friend whose car needs repairs—can be helpful. Remember, it's not about feeling guilty for your own good fortune, but about reminding yourself that there are aspects of your life for which you can still be grateful.

6. *How can you leave a disturbing situation mentally?* Can you visualize a wall between yourself and the situation, physically walk away from the situation, or create blocks of time in which you will not focus on the situation, such as during your morning routine, during meals, or in the evenings? Can you imagine putting the situation in a box, closing it, and putting it away safely for some later time?

Once you've generated your list, make a point of engaging in at least one of these distracting activities a day. Record your favorite shows and keep crossword puzzle books around so that you always have access to a brief distraction. When you notice your stress level getting high, give yourself a break.

Soothe Your Senses

All too often, in the midst of stressful life events, people begin to neglect the very things that will help them get through the day. It is essential to be kind and compassionate toward yourself when you are experiencing distressing life changes. You may be focused on caring for others and so have put yourself last, getting so busy that you neglect self-care or simply don't notice that you are missing this essential ingredient to tolerating difficult circumstances.

Don't expect others to do this for you. It would be nice if other people understood your needs and emotions and were able to help you calm down and take a break. However, the ability to create calming and relaxing experiences for yourself is essential to getting through tough days. You can ease your way through life changes by being kind to yourself and giving yourself some comfort. Regularly soothing yourself makes you less vulnerable to extreme emotions and better able to cope.

PRACTICE: SELF-SOOTHE ASSESSMENT

As with the Distract Assessment, the goal here is to generate a list of activities. In this assessment, based on a DBT strategy to comfort and nurture yourself, you focus on the senses (Linehan 1993b). Brainstorm a list for each of the questions in the assessment. It may be helpful to organize your list into activities that focus on each of the five senses: hearing, vision, taste, touch, and smell.

1. Remember a time when you felt relaxed and unworried. You might think of a time at the beach, a lazy Saturday in bed, or a vacation. What were the sensations that you were experiencing? Could you see a beautiful view? Were you snuggled under soft covers? Was there relaxing music or good food? Make a list of all the calming physical sensations you can remember from this time.

2. What are ways that you like others to soothe you? Do you enjoy massages, a clean or well-decorated house, or a home-cooked meal? Think of how you can comfort yourself in ways that others have provided comfort to you in the past.

3. What are some comforts from childhood?

4. What's your favorite meal? What is its texture, look, and smell?

5. What's your favorite calming song, band, or music?

6. What items do you keep around the house that pamper and soothe? Do you have special lotions, a tub to soak your feet, a massage pillow, candles, or soft blankets?

7. Nature improves mood and can create a sense of calm. Describe what you find relaxing and comforting in nature. Focus on all

your senses in your description. Do you find that you unwind with the sound of rain on the roof, the scent of freshly cut grass, the feel of digging in the soil or in mounds of freshly fallen snow, or the taste of freshly picked apples?

Giving yourself permission to unwind is not a luxury; rather it is essential to your ability to continue to function, adjust to new circumstances, make important decisions, and care for the people and problems in your life. Now is a time to allow yourself a few guilty pleasures, without the guilt.

To get started, make some changes to your environment that increase opportunities to calm and soothe yourself. If you love the creaminess of a certain ice cream, buy it and allow yourself to enjoy it. Use a favorite scented lotion and let its smell calm you all day. Wear a silk shirt that feels soft and smooth. Put a picture from your last vacation out on your work desk. Get outside and listen to the breeze in the trees. Create playlists on your MP3 player of calming and soothing music.

If you're someone who has trouble giving yourself a break, then it's important to schedule activities into your day that help you unwind. Some people are natural caretakers and focus on alleviating the difficulties others face. If that is you, give yourself permission to turn that caretaking onto yourself. It's not selfishness. In fact, the ability to care for yourself is a strength that enables you to navigate through stressful times. If the oxygen masks deploy on an airplane, you are instructed to put on your own mask first before helping others. The logic is simple: you cannot help others if you don't have the strength and enough air to breathe. Use that same logic here. Incorporate soothing activities into every day because they are your oxygen. To function through stressful life events, you must care for yourself. And if you are well cared for, other people in your life will also benefit.

Improve Body and Mind

The skills in this chapter are not about trying to change the circumstances that are creating stress, but you can change how you are thinking about and responding to those circumstances. The strategies in this section are based on DBT skills that replace immediate negative reactions in your body and mind with more positive responses (Linehan 1993b). These strategies focus on calming your body's stress response and changing your outlook on the pain and distress in your life.

Calm Your Body's Stress Response

The body and mind are connected. The body communicates to and influences the mind and vice versa. When you're anxious and your mind is racing or stuck in worried thoughts, your body—because it is connected to your mind—is also uptight and tense. Sometimes the best way to improve your mind-set is to begin by calming your body.

PRACTICE: RELAXATION TECHNIQUES

When you relax the body, the mind slows and relaxes as well. The strain of one intensely stressful event or multiple stressors can make navigating the hassles of daily life overwhelming. When you're in crisis, activities that you accomplished in the past without difficulty, such as organizing your work space, dealing with lower-level work priorities, paying bills, maintaining your car, or going to the grocery store can suddenly trigger strong emotions, making the pressure feel unbearable. The following relaxation techniques, which include progressive relaxation, imagery, taking a minibreak, and being present in the moment, are designed to help you slow down, calm yourself, take a break, and focus scattered and anxious thinking.

PROGRESSIVE RELAXATION

Progressive relaxation involves systematically tensing and then untensing groups of muscles in your body, one by one.

1. Find a quiet time during the day when you won't be disturbed for a few minutes. Begin by shifting your attention to your face. Contract the muscles and hold them for three to five seconds and then relax.

2. Move slowly down through your body—neck, shoulders, back, abdomen, legs, and feet—contracting, holding, and relaxing the muscle groups as you go.

It's sometimes difficult to relax tensed muscles. You may not even be aware that certain muscles groups are stiff and strained. By first tensing your muscles, as in this exercise, you are better able to untense and relax them.

BUILDING A RELAXING IMAGE

Imagery can be used to distract, soothe, and increase your courage and confidence. You can use it to create a safe and secure place in your mind or to envision coping in effective ways when you encounter stress.

1. Find a quiet time during the day when you won't be disturbed. You can choose any time that works for you, such as in the evening, before bed, over a lunch break, or in the morning before getting started on your day. Think of a setting that you typically find relaxing. Relaxation imagery is often built around a meadow, mountain, or water (beach, ocean, or lake) scene, but it's okay to choose any relaxing place or scene you like.

2. Focus on your breath and slowing your breathing. You may want to close your eyes.

3. Imagine yourself approaching the setting you have chosen on a path. Begin to supply details for the path. Think about what you see, feel, hear, and smell. Is the sky blue, does a warm breeze brush your shoulders, do you hear the crunch of your steps on pebbles, or can you smell the salt from the sea or the scent of pine trees?

4. Now imagine arriving at the relaxing setting. Imagine walking for a bit, and think of calm and comforting physical sensations. Imagining details, like the caw of a seagull, the sound of lake water gently lapping at the shore, and the warmth of the sun on your cheeks will help you immerse yourself in the image.

5. Get comfortable in the image and allow yourself a few minutes to imagine sitting calmly and noticing the scene around you. Experience being relaxed, totally and completely, for three to five minutes and then imagine slowly rising and returning down the path.

6. Give yourself a few deep breaths before refocusing and returning to daily activities.

IMAGERY TO COPE AND CREATE CONFIDENCE

You can imagine how you would cope effectively when you encounter stress. This exercise is most helpful if you engage as many of your senses as you can during the process. Focus on your senses to bring colors, sounds, and smells to your image.

1. The first three to four times you do this exercise, you will want to find a quiet time during the day when you won't be disturbed for three to five minutes. With practice, you may imagine responding to circumstances effectively *during* times of stress. The image will come more easily the more you practice.

2. Identify a time when you need to cope with stressful circumstances. Singling out a specific moment, such as when you have to make a presentation at work, when your partner is critical, or when you're tired and dealing with multiple demands will help you create an effective image.

3. Imagine yourself in the situation and create a vision that makes you feel that you handled the situation with skill or confidence. For example, if you tend to yell when you're criticized, imagine yourself taking a few deep breaths and calmly responding to the criticism without either defensiveness or submission. Imagine how you would position your body. What body posture or body language would convey calm, openness, and confidence? Imagine yourself in that posture. Form the specific words you would say in your mind or envision distancing yourself from the stressor and finding a way to self-soothe. What specific strategy would you use? Incorporate it into your image.

4. As you become practiced at imagining this image, use it during times of stress. It may help you to behave with greater calm and confidence or to remember to use strategies to distance or soothe yourself.

With this strategy, you can replace habitual self-limiting responses with images of yourself coping effectively.

MINIBREAK

Everyone needs a vacation. During times of acute stress, the need to retreat and allow yourself to be taken care of is more intense. Unfortunately these times are often the worst time to take a break. The strategy of taking a minibreak is about taking small, planned breaks from stress and crisis. To take a break that doesn't create more problems for you, you must plan it in advance and return to your life when it's over.

• *Carl's Story (continued)*

On his commute to his brother's hospital, Carl passed several exits to local vacation spots. As he passed them, he frequently had a strong urge to simply turn off the road, head toward a vacation cottage, and not look back. Carl knew that he had to deal with his responsibilities and the reality of his life every day. At the same time, it was important that his need for escape didn't become so intense that he did one day just turn off that highway and run from his life.

Carl decided that once a week he would turn off the highway. He didn't head for a vacation cottage, but he did spend an hour in a bookstore, reading magazines and drinking coffee. It was not a week of relaxation and fun, but it was a brief respite from the stress of his daily life.

During difficult times, it's particularly important to think ahead and plan some minibreaks in your life. By doing so, you're less likely to impulsively take unplanned or lengthy breaks from your responsibilities, which can cause additional stressors.

1. In your journal or on a piece of paper, make a list of what you can do to take a break or a brief retreat. How can you allow yourself to be taken care of for the moment? You may not be able to get away for a week, but you may be able to stay in bed for a day, get a massage, or sit in the sun.

2. If work pressures have you stressed out, you might create mini-breaks from work by assigning work-free times and zones in your life. Make certain areas of the house, such as the dinner table or the couch, off limits for checking work e-mail or using the computer. Schedule daily or weekly blocks of time, such as dinner time and the hour after, Sunday afternoons, or lunchtimes that will be a break from thinking about work activities.

Remember to return to experiencing and dealing with your life after the break. It's healthy to take a break and regroup, but a minibreak can have destructive consequences if you don't return from it to deal with your life.

BE PRESENT IN THE MOMENT

Organizing your desk, dealing with nonurgent tasks on the job, and doing household chores are daily hassles that can build up and create mental clutter and additional stress in your life. However, with a different approach, they can become a way to focus the mind and reduce stress. Do you clean the house just to get it done so that you have time to do what you need or would like to do? Or do you clean the house to clean the house? The distinction may seem unimportant or sort of silly. But it is, in fact, a central concept in practicing being present in everyday life.

• *Carl's Story (continued)*

In his new position, Carl received a large amount of documentation that was not urgent but was important to his job. He saw dealing with the paperwork as something he had to finish so that he could get to all the things he wanted and needed to do. He'd throw papers into piles and stuff folders into desk drawers as he raced to get these things out of his way. All the while, he'd be making to-do lists in his head. He saw dealing with documentation as a task to get done so he would have time for other things, and he found it irritating and frustrating.

However, Carl discovered if he focused his entire attention on organizing and nothing else—no lists, no thoughts about getting through it, no planning for what he'd do immediately after—it became soothing instead of tiresome. When he focused entirely on just the one thing in the moment, he found satisfaction in clearing off his desk and creating a logical place for items he would need in the future. Instead of finishing anxious to race on to his to-do list, he finished calm and relaxed. His list of responsibilities was still waiting for him. He'd lost no time, but he'd experienced satisfaction and pleasure while organizing his desk and hadn't added to his stress by trying only to get through it and move on to the next thing.

Although it may seem counterintuitive, focusing your entire attention on everyday tasks, even those tasks that are irritating, can turn them into soothing and relaxing experiences.

1. To change a chore or daily routine into a relaxing moment, consider those tasks you rush through or avoid every day. Choose one and try to be fully present while you're doing it.

2. Give yourself some extra time to complete the task and move slowly through it, attending to the movement of your body and your physical sensations as you do it.

3. Be fully in the present moment with your body and your thoughts. If you find you're worrying, ruminating, or planning, simply bring your mind to the task at hand. It may be helpful to focus on your senses such as the warmth of the water as you wash dishes or the hum and vibration of the vacuum cleaner.

4. Throughout the day, try immersing yourself in other simple tasks and smaller duties. You can bring your fully present attention to almost any activity.

When you're stressed and faced with negative changes, it's difficult to become engrossed in activities and routines that seem trivial. But it is possible to find peace and calm in the present moment.

Improve Your Mind-Set

The emotional pain and suffering associated with crisis and stressful life events can shatter your sense of purpose and meaning. Crisis and painful experiences, such as the loss of a way of life, a trauma, the loss of a child, or health problems can leave you feeling as though you have no purpose. These experiences can challenge basic assumptions you've held about yourself and the world. When circumstances are no longer benign or predictable, you may lose a sense of security. In the midst of stress and crisis, you may be feeling vulnerable. Feelings of grief, sadness, fear, anger, and thoughts like *Why me?* are all common reactions to adverse circumstances.

FINDING MEANING

The ability to make sense of trauma, pain, and stress can help you to adapt to new life circumstances. Finding meaning can aid your adjustment to painful life events (Updegraff, Silver, and Holman 2008). Meaning does not change the event, but it does change how you perceive the event. This change can decrease symptoms of stress and improve your ability to cope. Even in the case of everyday, mundane stressors, finding meaning can decrease the emotional impact.

Every individual finds meaning in different and personal ways. Some find it helpful to uncover a positive consequence of a situation. Others find meaning in their social connections or faith or prayer. How you cope with stress has an impact on your ability to find meaning in your circumstances. Avoidance, denial, and engaging in problem behaviors decreases the likelihood that you will find meaning. Coping strategies such as finding social support, focusing on being in the present, and reinterpreting the event may help you find meaning.

PRACTICE: STRATEGIES TO FIND MEANING

The strategies in this practice are designed to help you regain your mental equilibrium. They include strategies to search for positive consequences in your circumstances and to seek social support. Those strategies, along with finding solace in prayer and spirituality and engaging in positive self-talk can help reconcile the adversity you are facing with your view of the world. One or two of these strategies may help put your situation in context, while others may not be as effective for you. Practice those strategies that work best to help you make sense of difficult times.

SEARCH FOR POSITIVE CONSEQUENCES

The following are questions to help you find the potential positive outcomes of distressing circumstances. You can think about these questions or jot down your thoughts about them in a journal or on a blank piece of paper.

- What good do you hope will come out of this difficult or painful situation?

- What are your hidden strengths and inner resources?

- How can you find compassion for yourself and for others, even for people who have caused you stress and pain? How can you face the situation with courage and dignity?

- What actions would be courageous and dignified?

- How do you want to be and live in this situation?

- Who are the people that are important to you?

- Whom and what do you value?

After you have answered these questions, use your answers to choose two to three ways you will approach this stressful situation. Think about specific attitudes, thoughts, and actions that may reduce your emotional distress.

Approaching a painful situation with a belief that something positive may come of it does not change your circumstances, but it does change how you feel about yourself and your ability to cope.

SEEK SOCIAL SUPPORT

Connecting with others can help you find joy and peace in the present moment and find meaning in your relationships with others. Choose two to three activities from the suggestions below to increase your social support.

- Seek advice from people you care about and respect and who you believe will help you find meaning.

- Reflect on those you care for and love.

- Reminisce with friends and loved ones.

- Engage in favorite activities with the people around you.

- Express to others how much you care for them.

- Celebrate holidays and special events.

- Ask for forgiveness if you've hurt others.

Connecting with others can reduce your sense of vulnerability, making the world seem less harsh.

PRAYER AND SPIRITUALITY

Prayer can be many things for many people. It can be a communion with a higher power, an openness or readiness for acceptance, a cry for help, or an expression of hope. It can hold our highest ideals and dearest wishes. Prayer can be part of a search for guidance, direction, and answers. It can be a method of seeking inner strength and wisdom and an invitation to bring something greater than ourselves into our lives.

If prayer has been a part of your life or you believe it might be helpful to you now, incorporate it into your life. There is no one right way to pray. You can create a ritual around it, praying at a particular time of day and repeating one calming prayer. Or you can incorporate it into your life, using it to ask for guidance or express hope as you feel the need. You can also repeat rituals of prayer that have been helpful to you in the past.

It doesn't matter what your religion is or whether you are particularly religious at all. Prayer, even nonreligious prayer, can be a path to acceptance. You do not have to pray to a religious entity; it can be a prayer to self, a loved one, nature, the world, something larger outside of yourself, or a higher power. Prayer is not for everyone, and it's okay if you don't want to try it.

SUPPORTIVE SELF-TALK

Instead of allowing your mind to fill with guilt, self-doubt, and worry, it can help to talk to yourself as if you were talking to a good friend whom you care about and believe in.

- Be your own cheerleader and make a conscious effort to replace the *I can't do it* or *It's too much* type of thinking with encouragement and positive self-talk.

- Make positive statements such as "I can do it," "It's going to be okay," "I can handle it," "I'm strong," "I'll get through it," and "I'll find a way."

- Imagine that you're speaking to a good friend. What would you say to support and encourage a friend through difficult times? It may be helpful to write it down and carry it around with you.

Stay On Track

Motivation to implement new strategies is essential to making any changes in your level of stress. Some of the strategies in this chapter may seem simple or like common sense, but if you don't use them, they won't work. It can be difficult to make even small changes when you're faced with adversity. Changing how you respond during times of stress and crisis requires that you alter habitual ways of reacting to stress. Automatic thinking and unhealthy routines are hard to interrupt. It takes conscious effort to make and maintain changes. When you're struggling emotionally, it's easy to get discouraged.

When your stress levels are low, create a plan you can use when your stress levels are high. Also think through the costs and benefits of using the plan before you're in the midst of a crisis; this way you'll use the strategies in this chapter that are most helpful for you.

PRACTICE: STRESS-SURVIVAL PLAN

Everyone has to tolerate some amount of pain and stress in life. The strategies in this chapter are designed to help you endure those painful and stressful moments that you can't change.

1. Look back through your notes from the practice exercises in this chapter.

2. Write out the heading "Stress-Survival Plan" and under it, list the following:

- Your top-ten methods of distracting yourself, from the Practice: Distract Assessment

- Your top-ten methods of self-soothing, from the Practice: Self-Soothe Assessment

- The three to five most effective methods for you to improve how your body and mind are responding to external stressors

3. Keep these strategies in mind so you can use them during times of stress.

We all have to accept and tolerate difficulties, stress, painful feelings, and distressing life events, but doing it well, without creating additional problems, can be very difficult. It is essential to have many strategies to use to get through difficult moments. Having a readily available list of strategies that are specific to you means you'll likely have the tools to manage your stress effectively when you need them.

Wrap-Up

Coping with crisis, trauma, and life changes without falling into destructive behaviors can be difficult. This chapter focused on the short-term, concrete, and practical strategies needed to tolerate and survive life's upheavals. They include creating distance from problems and adversity, being kind and gentle toward yourself, and improving both your body's reaction to stress and your mind-set about stressful circumstances.

CHAPTER 5

Improving Relationships

Relationships are a part of every aspect of our lives. The families we're born into shape and define our early growth and learning. A constellation of relationships describes who we are as adults: mother, father, aunt, uncle, son, daughter, wife, husband, partner, employee, manager, boyfriend, girlfriend, landlord, friend, rival. Even when we are lonely, our feelings of loneliness stem from a deficiency in our relationships.

Relationships and Stress

Both conflicted relationships and isolation from others create stress and anxiety and can affect all aspects of your life. Disagreement can lead to productive change, but unresolved conflict can result in fractured relationships, regret, loneliness, anger, aggravation, hostility, and, ultimately, strain and stress.

While conflicted relationships can create stress, the symptoms of stress can add to relationship strain. When you completed your stress log in the first chapter, you may have noticed that too much emotion, worry, or rumination can get in the way of your ability to interact effectively with others. When you're stressed, you're more vulnerable to intense and sometimes painful feelings such as anger, anxiety, or frustration. At the same time, you may worry about things such as guilty feelings, how asserting yourself will impact others, or how others will respond to you. The intensity of your feelings and worries can overwhelm your ability to interact effectively.

Although you cannot control the behavior of those with whom you have relationships, you can improve your own ability to negotiate the ups and downs inherent in your social world. It is possible to change how you interact. When interactions change, you can alter the quality of your relationships—and your ability to get what you want and need—while maintaining the relationship and your self-respect. Steps to reduce stress within your relationships include the following:

- Understand your typical approach to social interactions.

- Balance those things that are important to you with the demands of others.

- Change how you interact with others.

In DBT, maintaining and improving relationships is considered a skill that can be learned. DBT teaches assertiveness, listening, and communication skills to improve how you make requests, respond to the demands of others, and maintain your values (Linehan 1993b).

Your Approach to Social Interactions

Before looking at changing your responses in interpersonal situations, explore your typical style of reacting to others. According to Robert Alberti and Michael Emmons (1978), your responses to others can be classified in three categories: *assertive, aggressive, and nonassertive:*

- *Assertive responses*, which are typically direct, forthright, respectful, and caring, are considered the most effective type of response for getting your wants and needs met. A good feeling often, but not always, accompanies assertive responses (Alberti and Emmons 1978).

- In contrast, *aggressive responses*, often meant to help us achieve our goals, do so at the expense of others, resulting in strained and conflicted relationships. For instance, an aggressive supervisor's response at work would be to yell at or belittle a subordinate any time she perceived a mistake had been made.

- *Nonassertive responses*, characterized by submission to others, tend to leave you feeling resentful, lonely, or distant from others. A nonassertive supervisor is likely to ignore mistakes, try to be friends with employees, and never clearly articulate what he needs from subordinates. Whether at work or in your personal life, these two styles of interacting can result in greater amounts of strain in your relationships.

Your style of social interaction can be situational. It can change with context, people, and emotions. When you are feeling stressed, you may respond quite differently to a situation or person than when you are calm. You might generally be direct and articulate but, when overwhelmed, find you have a short fuse or are capitulating to other people rather than standing up for yourself.

PRACTICE: INTERPERSONAL SKILLS ASSESSMENT

The following questions are based on DBT skills designed to help you improve your communication skills (Linehan 1993b). The intent is to get you thinking about your own style of responding in interpersonal situations. This exercise is not a personality test and won't give you a personality type; however, it will help you determine your tendency to relate passively, aggressively, or directly with others. And it may show you how the way you relate differs in different social situations.

Find a quiet time during the day and take out your journal or a blank piece of paper. Rate your level of agreement with the following statements on a scale of 1 (rarely, with great difficulty) to 7 (all the time, easily). An answer of 4 means you respond this way some of the time, with a moderate amount of difficulty.

1. *Situational assertiveness.* The following statements are designed to help you begin to determine whether your style of relating to others differs from one context to the next. Rate your level of agreement with each statement on a scale from 1 to 7.

   a. I ask for what I want and need in all types of relationships (e.g., in romantic relationships, with family and friends, and with strangers, such as waitresses, car attendants, or store clerks).

b. I ask for what I want and need regardless of my emotions. For example, I'm able to assert myself when I'm overwhelmed, under pressure, anxious, disappointed, happy, or in love.

c. I ask for what I want and need regardless of the importance of my request. For example, I'm able to ask for small favors as well as those things that are extremely important to me.

Most people will see some variation in how they interact with others. Look over your answers; note whether you have lower numbers. Lower numbers indicate that your response varies based on context.

2. *Nonassertive style.* The following questions are designed to help you begin to determine your style of responding to others. If you noticed from the questions above that your style varies significantly depending on the context, you may want to answer these questions more than once, each time within a different context (e.g., type of relationship, level of emotion, or importance of request) in mind.

a. I am always in tune with the wants and needs of others around me.

b. I often go along with others, even if I disagree with them.

c. I tend to judge myself.

d. I feel guilty when I ask for things from others.

e. I worry about how other people will react when I ask for something or say no to them.

f. I don't tell people when my feelings are hurt.

g. I often find that resentments and problems have built up.

h. I try to accommodate all the demands of others.

i. I do what I should, even when there is something else I want to be doing.

j. I frequently apologize for myself or my beliefs.

k. I lie rather than confront someone.

l. I am criticized for being indecisive.

3. *Aggressive style.* Aggressive communication is a style of interaction aimed at getting your feelings and opinions heard and your needs met. However, aggressive communication can involve intimidation, attempts to control others, violating the rights of others, and possibly being physically or emotionally abusive.

   a. I need to get my way or "win" arguments.

   b. I am often in conflict with others.

   c. I have trouble giving up a disagreement, even when the other person wants to drop it.

   d. I believe that there are certain ways of interacting that everyone should follow.

   e. I tend to lose my cool.

   f. I use threats, verbal attacks, or name calling when angry.

   g. I have trouble tolerating a "no" to a request.

4. *Assertive style.* Assertive communication is a style of advocating for your needs and expressing opinions and feelings in an open and direct manner. Assertive communication is respectful to the points of view of others and, at the same time, lets you be candid about your own limitations, needs, and perspective.

   a. If I have an emotional reaction, I can articulate what I'm reacting to.

   b. I'm able to express my feelings and opinions without becoming overly emotional.

   c. I ask for what I want and need.

   d. I'm willing to negotiate to get my needs met.

   e. I'm usually polite and considerate.

   f. I listen to other points of view.

   g. I make eye contact when speaking to others.

   h. I'm aware of my values and beliefs and I voice them when needed.

   i. I ask people to do their fair share.

5. Look over your answers; note where you have the highest numbers. Answers closer to a rating of 7 indicate a way you approach interactions. Now add the numbers for each section above to see which total is the highest. Sections with a higher rating indicate a regular style of interaction for you. If you have the highest numbers in the nonassertive section, you may be more passive than others in how you interact with people. You might be likely to put other people's needs before your own and find yourself overloaded with the demands of others or with built-up hurts or resentments. If your answers tend toward a higher rating in the aggressive section, consider that you are more forceful in how you interact with others. You might find that people take offense, that you have frequent misunderstandings with others, or that relationships are strained and characterized by frequent conflict.

Social interactions are complicated and constantly shifting, which can make responding in different situations challenging. By identifying your main approach to interactions, you can begin to focus on those communication skills that come less naturally to you.

This chapter is about developing skills to improve the interactions that cause you stress. The focus is on improving in areas where you struggle and on resolving problems and misunderstandings before they build up and become overwhelming.

Balance

Relating to others isn't just about connection and social support; it's also about getting what you want and need in order to better manage your life. Much of the strain that occurs in relationships arises when your wants and priorities conflict with your own internalized social rules or with what someone else demands of you.

DBT teaches that to manage interpersonal strain, you must know and prioritize your wants and needs and negotiate with others to put off low-priority demands, communicate your needs, and say no to unwanted requests (Linehan 1993b).

Identifying Your Wants vs. Shoulds and Your Priorities vs. Demands

Wants are things you desire. Wants can make life fun and interesting. You might want to spend time with friends, have time for a hobby, or take a vacation. *Shoulds*, on the other hand, are your internal obligations and expectations. These may have been external expectations, moral codes, or rules that you internalized long ago that have now become pressures you place on yourself. For example, you may have internalized certain rules about work interactions or responding to phone messages. You may have internal rules about household chores or social obligations that conflict with what you want to do. For instance, you may feel you should help your partner with the dishes, but you want to surf the Internet; you may feel you should write thank-you notes, but you want to watch TV. You can think of your wants and shoulds as weights on opposite ends of a balance (Linehan 1993b).

Priorities are those things that are of most value to you, that you consider an important part of living a fulfilling life, and, in particular, that will allow *you* to live a life that is fulfilling to *you* rather than one that is meaningful to someone else. Your priorities might include getting an education, expressing yourself creatively, or doing meaningful work.

Demands are those things you have to do. They are expectations and requirements that society and other people place on you. They might include paying bills and taxes, getting your state-mandated car inspection, wearing clean clothes, picking up after yourself, or completing certain tasks at work (Linehan 1993b).

PRACTICE: IDENTIFYING WANTS AND SHOULDS, PRIORITIES AND DEMANDS

Wants, shoulds, priorities, and demands are highly individual; they are determined by your personality, your culture, your past experiences, and the circumstances of your life.

1. Find a quiet time during the day and take out your journal or a blank piece of paper and create a table with two columns. Label one column "Wants" and the other "Shoulds."

2. Call to mind a particularly stressful or overwhelming situation as the focus for this exercise. For instance, at work you may feel you have too much work and unresolved conflicts and employees who aren't productive. Under the "Wants" column, list activities that you find pleasurable and things that you wish for or desire. In the example, you would focus on the aspects of your job that you enjoy or find pleasurable. Under the "Shoulds" column, make a list of your internal expectations of yourself. Include expectations you grew up with or that you internalized as a child, such as cultural or family expectations. In the example of a stressful work situation, you might identify internal expectations about your work ethic, the quality of your relationships with people at work, or the quality of your work.

3. Now make two more columns, this time labeled "Priorities" and "Demands." As you did with the "Wants" and "Shoulds" columns, make a list underneath each heading of your priorities and the external demands that you face.

Setting Goals to Attain Balance

When you carry around a heavy load of internal rules—shoulds—you become worn down and burdened by your own expectations. Similarly, regularly putting other people's demands before your own priorities leaves you overwhelmed and stressed by numerous tasks but without the fulfillment that comes from focusing on your own priorities.

To create balance, you must articulate your own wants and priorities, respond to your own important shoulds and the high-priority demands of others, and negotiate to put off or unload other people's lower-priority demands.

PRACTICE: EXAMINING WANTS VS. SHOULDS, PRIORITIES VS. DEMANDS

1. Imagine that each "want" you've identified is a weight on a balance and each "should" is a weight on the other side of the

balance. Is one side heavier than the other? Are you attending to one side more than the other? Is the weight on one side of the balance so heavy that it is close to the breaking point?

2. Now do this same imaginal exercise with your priorities and demands. As you view your priorities and demands on a balance, ask yourself whether the scale is unbalanced.

   a. *Examining the balance.* When you did the imaginal exercise, did you find it out of balance? Do you have too many shoulds? Too many demands?

   b. *Too many shoulds and demands.* If your own wants and priorities are getting sidelined, look at your list and identify the lower-priority shoulds and demands. You can use principles of dialectical thinking in chapter 2 and acceptance strategies in chapter 3 to change how you approach your own internal "shoulds" that are creating unnecessary stress in your life. For example, you might want to practice letting go of thoughts that you "must" behave in certain ways or that you are "bad" if you relax your standards for yourself (as described in chapter 2). Or you might use strategies to get your body into a more accepting state (see chapter 3) when you find yourself pressuring yourself with these shoulds. There are also methods to put off or unload other people's lower-priority demands; you will want to focus on the strategies in the "Obtaining Change" section (later in this chapter) to learn how to articulate what's best for you and negotiate with others to move these lower-priority demands off your list.

The level of demands varies in life. At certain times in your life, such as when you've just had a baby, started a new job, or experienced a health crisis, your ability to attend to the demands of others and to your internal shoulds will be out of balance with your ability to attend to your own priorities and wants.

But even in the midst of life-changing events and legitimate needs from the people around you, it is essential to remain aware of and attentive to your own wants and priorities. Internal pressures, external stressful events, and demands from others all contribute to the physical and emotional strain you experience.

Evaluating Priorities

You may be feeling overwhelmed by other people's demands but also be unsure about which to put off or when to ask for help. And if you're uncertain about your rights or unsure about the value of voicing your point of view, you may find yourself failing to act on your own behalf.

Will a small lie to cover a mistake erode self-respect? Will agreeing to take on extra responsibilities leave you chronically stressed out and emotionally reactive? Will you lose out on promotions or opportunities because you are not sure when to give voice to your accomplishments and future goals?

Having a method to evaluate your priorities can help you to act in your own best interests. The following exercise is based on DBT skills that help you evaluate whether to assert yourself (Linehan 1993b).

You can think of assertiveness as occurring on a spectrum with insisting upon and demanding your rights at one end and not acting or addressing an issue in any way at all on the other end. In the middle, you'll find hinting, compromising, and asking firmly with an openness to negotiation.

How strongly you make your case is linked to your priorities, your rights, the quality of your relationship with the other person, and your goals. Unfortunately, you can't reduce a social situation to a few questions that will, without fail, determine the best course of action. However, when you're uncertain how to proceed, it can help to think through your priorities, the nature of your relationship with the other person, and your short- and long-term needs.

PRACTICE: DECIDING HOW STRONGLY TO ASSERT YOURSELF

1. Pick one interaction with someone from the past week in which you were uncertain how to proceed. You may have said nothing, been uncertain of whether it was appropriate to bring up a concern, said yes when you wanted to say no, or brushed off a problem you had, telling yourself that it wasn't important.

2. Find a quiet time during the day and take out your journal or a blank piece of paper and describe the situation, sticking to the facts as much as possible. Use "I" statements in your description such as "I want," "I think," or "I feel" to clarify the situation. Be on the lookout for judgmental words such as "should" and "fair" and try to replace them with a description of the situation or how the situation makes you feel.

3. Once you feel that you've clearly articulated the situation, rate your level of agreement with each statement for this situation on a scale of 1 (yes, strongly agree) to 7 (no, strongly disagree). A rating of 4 would be balanced in the middle:

   a. I have enough information to make a decision. I am not trying to decide based on partial knowledge.

   b. There are laws or moral codes that require me to get what I want or need from this situation.

   c. I can say no and still respect the other person's values and rights.

   d. I have a reciprocal relationship with this person.

   e. I give more than I get in this relationship.

   f. Keeping the peace now will create problems in the long run. For example, if I avoid conflict to keep the relationship as it is right now, will I compromise my self-respect, lose out on opportunities, or feel resentful in the long term?

4. Look back over your answers to the questions above. Were the answers to these questions closer to a 1 or a 7? If they were closer to a 1, consider asserting yourself in this situation. If they were closer to a 7, shift toward not doing anything. If they tended to be in the middle, you will want to focus on negotiating and compromising.

Completing the questions above helps you clarify how strongly to assert your wants or needs. Once you determine whether to assert yourself, you will need to consider who has the ability to give you what you want or need and to choose an occasion to make your request.

Changing Your Interactions

To reduce the stress you experience from strained relationships, it's essential to change some of the ways you interact with others. Learning and using skills to assert your needs, negotiate, listen, empathize effectively with others, and stand up for your beliefs can decrease negative emotion and stress. There are specific ways that you can interact with others that can improve the quality of your relationships. In DBT, interpersonal skills training combines social skills training (McKay, Davis, and Fanning 2009), listening skills (Barker 1971), and assertiveness training (Alberti and Emmons 1978).

• *Nissa's Story*

Nissa is a thirty-eight-year-old accountant. At twenty-six she landed a job at a big firm. Because she was young and inexperienced, Nissa gave way to her coworkers when making decisions about how to handle loopholes or changes in regulations, and in daily decisions about such things as work hours and which projects she'd be involved in. After making a small mistake early on, she became even more passive. When she disagreed with coworkers' decisions or work style, she would concede to them to keep the peace. She frequently told herself that they were more experienced and better trained, so it was not her place to question them.

Nissa stayed with the company for many years, but over time, her style of interacting with coworkers didn't change and she became angry and resentful as coworkers who she felt were less qualified were promoted above her. She began to dread going to work and found herself passively letting others take credit for work she had contributed to and using sarcasm and name calling to denigrate her coworkers. She felt like she wasn't herself at work. Ultimately she left the company for a position at a different company.

Nissa didn't know how to stand up for herself, take credit for her accomplishments, ask for help when she needed it, or assert her point of view about important work issues. Not knowing what to do or how to handle a situation can cause misunderstanding, conflict, and tension in relationships—all of which increase your stress levels.

Obtaining Change: Asking for What You Need and Saying No

If you're like many people, you find it is easy to be polite, direct, and honest in some situations, such as when you're calm and surrounded by people you like and care about. However, in other situations, it can be extremely difficult to candidly express how you feel, such as when you're hurt, angry, worried about negative consequences, or dealing with someone who you feel doesn't respect your opinion. These are the times that you need a strategy to act with assertiveness rather than with passivity or aggression.

In Linehan's skills manual, she outlines how to communicate in ways that improve understanding and maintain long-term relationships (Linehan 1993b).

WHAT YOU SAY

Prepare the listener for your request by giving some background and describing the facts. Avoid emotionally laden and judgmental words such as "should," "fair," "unfair," "right," "wrong," or "stupid." Instead describe the situation using data and statements about how you feel.

For example, during a disagreement about the assignment of a work project in a new job, Nissa prepared her supervisor, Tom, for a request by saying, "Since I started, I've spent much of my time working on routine, uncomplicated projects. I haven't had the opportunity to work on a more complicated project, which I find energizing and I really enjoy. I'm feeling like my skills are underutilized, which is frustrating." Directly speak out and ask for what you want. Make your request or your answer to the other person's request clear. At the same time, focus on the positive. Often situations have desirable features for both people involved. Be sure to articulate those positives in your request.

In Nissa's case, she continued the discussion with Tom by saying, "I'd like to be assigned to this new project that has interesting features, which I have the ability to handle. By taking on the more complicated project, I could ease your load a bit, since you've been working long hours lately."

Nissa knew that Tom valued her happiness at work and her productivity. He also had been struggling to balance long work hours with family expectations. By articulating those positive outcomes, she increased the likelihood that he would respond positively to her request.

HOW YOU SAY IT

Be aware of your body language. Make eye contact. Keep your voice level, and have a relaxed but confident posture—no slumped shoulders or clenched fists. Be honest and direct. If the conversation is veering away from your goal, bring it back. Allow room for the other person to communicate his or her point of view. Negotiate. In Nissa's case, rather than getting stuck in a rigid position about her role on one specific work project, she listened to Tom's concerns about her abilities to handle the new project and negotiated. In the end, Tom agreed that Nissa would be a part of the project she was interested in, with some limitations around her responsibilities, and Nissa agreed to continue to take on some of the less interesting projects in the future, with the understanding that if she performed well on this new project, she'd have more opportunities for challenging projects.

It's important to stand up for yourself, express how you feel, and get your needs met. When you know what to say and how to say it, you can get your wants and needs met while maintaining relationships.

PRACTICE: MAKING A REQUEST

1. Pick one interaction in the next week in which you want to make a request. Begin by choosing a situation that you feel will be relatively easy. For example, you may want to make a specific request at a restaurant, ask a loved one for a favor, or ask a coworker for assistance.

2. Make your request. Begin by preparing the listener, remembering to focus on facts and statements about how you feel. Then ask directly for what you want and articulate the positives for the other person.

3. If the other person states differing wants or needs, listen attentively and then suggest alternatives that come closer to meeting both of your needs.

Practicing approaching difficult situations with direct communication can help defuse differences of opinion, increase the likelihood that you will get what you need, and improve long-term relationships.

Improving the Quality of Relationships

Earlier in the chapter, you completed an exercise about your typical style of interacting in interpersonal situations. If you discovered that you often act aggressively to get your needs met, you may need to focus on skills to keep your relationships.

APPROACH WITH OPENNESS

Approaching others with openness and actively listening to their thoughts and concerns can make a significant difference in the strength and quality of your relationships. Approach others with compassion, consideration, and curiosity. Remember that there is no absolute truth, and be open to perspectives other than your own. Try to establish a comfortable and relaxed atmosphere when you interact. Notice your tone of voice, use of personal space, and body language.

Even if you feel someone has treated you poorly, don't attack or threaten them. Remain considerate as well as curious and interested in their point of view. Keep your thoughts, words, and tone of voice kind and moderate. When in doubt, be courteous. Use this same approach in the thoughts you direct at yourself. Maybe you've offended someone, spoken in anger, said things you didn't mean, or embarrassed yourself. Be kind and calm in your thoughts toward yourself. Self-recrimination will leave you feeling guilty and irritable and more likely to lash out defensively.

LISTEN EFFECTIVELY

To listen effectively, you need to acknowledge other people's feelings, struggles, and points of view. You don't have to agree with someone or believe that they are right in order to communicate to them that you understand how they are feeling. Sometimes all someone needs is to know that you hear them.

PRACTICE: ACTIVE LISTENING

1. Pick one interaction in the next week. Concentrate your physical and mental energy on listening. If you begin to think about your

response instead of listening, bring yourself back to the act of listening to the other person. Allow the person to finish speaking before you formulate a response. Listen for what is legitimate and compelling in any viewpoints that differ from your own.

2. Demonstrate to the person that you are listening. You can do this with your body language, by nodding, leaning toward the person, and making eye contact. You can demonstrate verbally by summarizing what the person is saying. When you respond, ask for clarification or reflect on what they have said to ensure that you have understood them.

When you listen actively, you can strengthen your relationships, identify commonalities, respond to full rather than partial communications, and reduce conflict, thereby reducing stress. When you actively listen to someone, they feel heard and understood, which can decrease emotional intensity when you're in conflict. It can also increase your understanding of another person's perspective, making it more likely that you will propose a course of action or compromise that is appealing to that person.

Keeping Your Self-Respect

We all smooth over the truth and bend in our standards or principles from time to time to reduce conflict and make relationships work. But if pleasing others becomes a habit and smoothing over disagreements and arguments becomes more important than your own personal beliefs, you may find that you're compromising your self-respect.

It's common to lose sight of your values slowly, over time. If you've had negative experiences with confrontation, you may behave like Nissa, with one concession leading to another until you feel unappreciated and resentful.

In Nissa's case, standing up for herself, knowing her values, and voicing them—as well as communicating her achievements and owning up to her own mistakes on a daily basis—required courage. She had to actively focus on maintaining her integrity and values in these daily interactions.

PRACTICE: RECONNECTING WITH LOST VALUES

To act with self-respect you must maintain your own values and beliefs while getting what you want and need in the world. To do this, act in ways that fit your values and make you feel competent and capable.

In DBT people are taught the skills to maintain self-respect (Linehan 1993b). And a key part of self-respect is to reconnect with what is important to you.

1. Think of a person whom you admire.

2. What is it that you admire about that person?

3. What specific qualities do they have that are admirable?

4. Which of their qualities, values, and actions would you like to emulate?

Nissa admired her sister. She had a stable career as a health services manager, expressed her opinions and emotions without aggression, listened to other people's points of view, and was giving and caring toward others while at the same time standing up for her own point of view and needs.

Sometimes we give in or behave in ways that get us what we want or need indirectly. We may lie, act helpless, or give in to someone else so we don't create an argument (Linehan 1993b). Although these things work to get us what we want and need, in the long run, they make us feel worse about ourselves. Using them every now and then won't have too big an effect, but using them often will.

PRACTICE: STICKING TO YOUR VALUES

1. Make a conscious effort over the next week to focus on sticking up for yourself and your beliefs without aggressively pushing your perspective on others.

2. Notice any urges to smooth over conflict with small lies or compromises on important beliefs or values. In those instances,

concentrate on being truthful and direct. This takes practice. It can be hard to articulate the truth or your own values, especially when you anticipate a negative reaction.

3. If you need to, practice first in interactions that feel more comfortable and with people who tend to be more open and forgiving.

If you typically approach situations nonassertively, you may have made a habit of avoiding conflict or getting what you need by making compromises to your values. Over time, you may find that you have compromised important values. Beginning to refocus on your values and relating to others honestly and directly can improve self-respect and reduce the stress and pressure of failing to get your own needs met.

Sometimes circumstances are out of your control, and you will be thwarted no matter how you approach a situation. It's important to understand that sometimes inequalities in the environment and power imbalances in society and certain relationships are not going to change, even when you change your way of interacting (Linehan 1993b). To keep your self-respect when faced with circumstances beyond your control, you have to consider other options, such as leaving a destructive relationship or recognizing power disparities and identifying other avenues for getting your needs met when a particular person can't or won't meet them.

Wrap-Up

As described in this chapter, all relationships require attention. Without relationship skills, we are unable to get the support that would help us manage stressful life events. And when we don't attend to our relationships, conflict and tension with people around us can become a significant source of stress. This chapter focused on knowing your own style of interacting with others, doing what is expected of you while maintaining focus on those things that give your life meaning and joy, and changing interactions that create stress in your life. It is important to develop good relationship skills to decrease the anguish, self-recrimination, built-up hurt, and misunderstandings that increase life strain and stress. Relationship skills are required to resolve conflict, get your legitimate needs met, and live in alignment with your values and beliefs.

CHAPTER 6

Cultivating Mindfulness

Mindfulness practice is about focusing your attention and cultivating a nonreactive awareness of your thoughts, physical experiences, and feelings so you can participate fully in the present moment. The practice can improve your physical and emotional well-being and enhance your ability to cope with stress.

Scattered, distracted, and self-critical reactions can perpetuate and intensify the negative emotions that are often a part of the stress response. Under stress you may find yourself in "automatic pilot" mode, reacting without thought, distracted by worry, and making hasty decisions. For example, that recurrent fight with your partner or the repeating problem at work is often a result of operating and responding out of habit rather than with thought or consciousness. When you are perpetually distracted or attached to habitual patterns of thinking and feeling, stress increases.

In an effort to reduce external pressures, you may feel compelled to take on multiple tasks at one time. Unfortunately, attempting to complete more and more at once—*multitasking*—doesn't lead to greater productivity or lower stress levels. In fact, in a study conducted by Stanford professors Eyal Ophir, Clifford Nass, and Anthony Wagner, people who routinely engaged in multitasking (for example, using the Internet or mobile phone and watching TV while performing other tasks) did worse on a series of tasks than those people who were low multitaskers (Ophir, Nass, and Wagner 2009). Multitasking decreases your ability to remember information or to filter out irrelevant material. And each time you switch from one task to another, there is a *switch cost*—the time it takes for your brain to switch from one task to another and then get up to speed on that task. The more complicated the task, the greater the switch cost. Inevitably, as the demands of the tasks you are trying to complete exceed your ability to accomplish them, stress increases.

When stressed, you're more vulnerable to intense and painful emotions. Self-criticism and judgmental thinking that often accompany stress intensify emotions such as anger, shame, and anxiety. In turn, the experience of intense painful emotions increases the perception of stress. Strong emotion can impair your ability to cope effectively and further distort your thinking about your circumstances.

When stressed, people often fall into unhealthy behaviors, such as smoking, overspending, over- or undereating, or drinking alcohol excessively. With DBT, we assume that these unhealthy behaviors are distractions, sometimes only brief distractions, from negative feelings (Linehan 1993a). The temporary relief from painful stress-related emotions that these distractions provide perpetuates these behaviors and makes it difficult to adopt healthier coping mechanisms.

Mindfulness exercises that promote focused attention and an awareness of emotions, without judgment or behavioral reaction, are designed to counteract automatic-pilot, scattered thinking, and unhealthy coping. In a review of recent research, Paul Grossman and colleagues found support for the physical and mental health benefits of mindfulness practice, which is shown to improve well-being, reduce stress and stress-related symptoms, and enhance coping with distress in everyday life (Grossman et al. 2004). Research indicates that mindfulness practice can stimulate changes in the brain by activating parts of the brain associated with positive mood (Davidson et al. 2003).

What Is Mindfulness?

The construct of *mindful awareness* originated in early Buddhist practice and is present in almost every religious tradition (Goleman 1977). Despite its origins in religious practice, mindfulness in DBT is a nonreligious skill designed to bring a particular quality of attention and awareness to your life. Mindfulness is characterized by unemotional, nonevaluative, and sustained moment-to-moment awareness. It is the examination of your internal and external world through the act of bringing calm and open attention to your thoughts, behaviors, feelings, and experiences. Today mindfulness is widely taught for the purpose of stress reduction.

Mindful Attention

In any given moment, we are all both mindful and mindless to one extent or another. Mindfulness is developing the capacity to bring your attention to all aspects of your life. Whether you are washing dishes, driving, worrying, laying back in the dentist chair, walking, meditating, or in a business meeting, mindful attention allows you to notice your experience in the moment. When you are mindful, you perceive your thoughts, physical state, emotions, and world the way they are, without judging the experience.

The quality of the attention that you bring to your experience is crucial. To practice mindfulness, you must let go of the evaluations of your thoughts, feelings, and experiences. To focus on the actuality of your experience, you need to suspend your judgments and expectations. When distractions, judgments, expectations, and evaluations occur during mindful practice, notice them as part of the moment and then bring your attention to the present.

The Concept of Wise Mind

In DBT, Linehan describes a state of mind she calls *wise mind*. *Wise mind* is an internal sense of knowing that comes from a combination of emotional experiencing and problem solving (1993a). Wise mind is both thoughtful and intuitive, emotional and rational.

Sometimes, despite our best efforts, we are faced with stressors beyond our control that elicit anger, frustration, and anxiety—for example, the dishwasher that overflows, a boss who yells, intense relatives, morning traffic, a broken air conditioner, a leaky roof, bills, and car trouble. These are stressors that we're generally unable to avoid.

Stressful daily hassles and difficult life events can trigger intense emotions when they interfere with the ability to reach goals. For example, if the traffic jam keeps you from a job interview, you may experience emotions such as panic, outrage, and exasperation. In the midst of these emotions, you're more likely to act impulsively—say, by yelling, lying, blaming and insulting others, stubbornly refusing to take necessary action, and causing yourself more trouble.

When you act with wise mind, you notice your judgments, intense emotions, and urges to act. You're able to step back from your emotional attachment to the circumstances of the situation, which allows you to expand your awareness beyond your own personal desires. Mindfulness practice improves your ability to respond to life as it is, rather than with self-limiting reactions, such as defensiveness, rationalization, or dismissiveness. When you are in wise mind, you can change your tactics if necessary, avoid needless conflict, and see options you didn't previously see.

Intentional and daily mindfulness practice can reconnect you with your wise mind. Studies of mindfulness continue to find that the practice leads to a greater sense of wisdom, self-efficacy, and insight (Carmody and Baer 2007).

Practicing Mindfulness

If you were to learn any new skill (say, playing the piano or downhill skiing), you would need to practice to achieve your goal of mastering the skill. Practice in mindfulness is different, however, than practicing other skills. It is not a rehearsal to master or achieve proficiency but rather a participation in the experience of the moment. Jon Kabat-Zinn, the founder of mindfulness-based stress reduction, describes mindful practice as simply engaging in the discipline of mindfulness in the present moment without a goal or expectation of any particular outcome (Kabat-Zinn 2003).

This practice can seem contradictory at times. Why engage in a practice that's intended to reduce stress but doesn't offer you the expectation or goal of stress reduction? In mindfulness, your practice is focused on the *process* of experiencing and participating in the present moment rather than in striving for an outcome. When you attach a goal or expectation to that experience, it pulls you out of the present moment to thoughts of the past or expectations for the future.

Although practicing mindfulness differs from learning other new skills, it is like any skill: learning to be mindful takes effort and repetition. You will find that as you repeat the exercises in this chapter, you become better able to attend to daily life without becoming distracted or caught up in thoughts or emotions. Because being fully present and attentive during moments of stress can be difficult, it's important to practice and become skilled during moments of relative calm. Attempts to learn new skills when under pressure are generally much less successful than during times of calm.

The practice of mindfulness involves engaging in formal exercises on a regular basis as well as informal mindful awareness of day-to-day life. This chapter provides *intentional* practice exercises (in which you will set time aside to focus on particular aspects of your experience) and mindfulness practices for everyday life (which aim to reduce stress by routinely bringing mindfulness into each day of your life).

Letting Go (Not Reacting to Inner Experience)

The intentional mindfulness exercises will require you to practice letting go of habitual ways of thinking and feeling. You may find when you first attempt these exercises that instead of focusing on the mindfulness practice, you spend the time as you would during any other quiet moment when stressed—ruminating, worrying, planning, or feeling anxious, sad, or ashamed.

Engaging in your usual patterns of thought and feeling is normal. But in these exercises, you will begin to develop the ability to notice when you are stuck in habitual stress-related thoughts and feelings. The act of noticing those thoughts and feelings as they occur creates distance and, with practice, will allow you to let those habitual responses go.

Nonevaluation of Experience

A central goal in DBT is to cultivate a nonjudgmental stance toward our lives and ourselves (Linehan 1993b). However, when we're stressed, it's difficult to refrain from passing judgment.

Judgments are the spontaneous and often inaccurate interpretations of our environment that influence our thinking and behavior. It's common to judge those who hurt us, conflict with us, or remind us of our shortcomings. Our harshest judgments are often those negative thoughts, such as *I'm lazy* or *I'm stupid*, that we've internalized about ourselves.

In each mindfulness practice in this chapter you will be instructed to notice distractions that pull you out of the moment. Begin to tune in to those distractions that come from your judgments or evaluations of your experience. Thoughts such as *This isn't worth my time*, *I'm bad at this*, *This is fantastic*, and *I should be able to do this* are all common judgments and evaluations of mindfulness practice. Becoming skilled at noticing judgments, expectations, and evaluations diminishes their ability to run your day-to-day life.

Many people confuse nonjudgmental thinking with trying to view events more positively. "Nonjudgment" is not about seeing the silver lining in difficult circumstances. Rather, it is about simply acknowledging the circumstances, feelings, or sensations without engaging in developing opinions or evaluating.

Being Present in the Moment

When you're stressed or anxious, it's easy to be engrossed in thoughts and worries about your stressful circumstances. Many people find that they go through daily routines such as showering, driving to work, or eating, so lost in thought that they barely remember experiencing them. It can be hard to pull yourself away from your worries and thoughts about other things to fully experience the present moment. Pressures to get things done can cause you to try to complete multiple tasks at once, and nervousness can leave you highly attuned to any distractions in the environment. Each of these disruptions can pull you away from the present moment and interfere with your ability to focus your attention.

During your mindfulness practice, resist the urge to multitask or be pulled from the activity by internal distractions or commotion in the environment around you. In both the intentional and the mindfulness practices in everyday life, practice focusing your mind and awareness on the current moment's activity rather than splitting your attention among several activities and thoughts. With time and practice, you will find you are better able to choose the focus of your attention. You will be able to notice and let interruptions pass, allowing you to remain present in the moment and in your life.

Intentional Mindfulness Practice

For each of these intentional mindfulness exercises below, you will want to find a quiet time when you will be uninterrupted for ten to fifteen minutes. To begin to gain control over your attention and cultivate awareness without distraction, it's best to practice daily. Some people find it helpful to set aside a certain time of the day in which to practice, such as first thing in the morning, just before bed, over a lunch break, or before dinner. When you're stressed and overwhelmed, it may feel like you don't have time to incorporate another activity into your day, but setting aside just a few quiet moments to practice these exercises can improve your focus and allow you to respond to the events of the day from a place of calm and centeredness.

The first few times you practice each exercise, you will need to read the instructions completely through before beginning the practice.

Once you've completed an exercise, consider for a moment what pulled you out of the exercise or distracted you. Take one to two minutes at the end of each practice and jot down in your journal or on a blank piece of paper those things that made it difficult to focus your attention. As you become aware of your distractions over time, you will be better able to notice them and let them pass as they occur during the practice.

Attending to Your Inner Experience

When stressed, we're often so consumed by external pressures that we disconnect from our internal world. Formal mindfulness practice helps you notice your internal experience and discover unexamined physical sensations, thoughts, and emotions.

PRACTICE: MINDFUL BREATHING

In this exercise, you will quiet your body and clear your mind using rhythmic breathing. Focusing on breathing can help when you're overwhelmed or your mind is wandering. You will tune in to your breath as it enters and leaves your body. The first few times you try this exercise, aim for the practice to last three to five minutes (it may help to set a timer so you don't have to worry about the time during the exercise). As you become more proficient at it, you can extend the time up to ten minutes (or more if you like).

1. If you choose to set a timer, do so at this point.

2. Begin by getting settled in a comfortable sitting position. It may be tempting to lie down, but this often makes it too easy to drift into sleep. You can sit in a comfortable chair or on the floor with your legs crossed.

3. Either gently close your eyes or find a focal point in front of you on which to focus your gaze. If you keep your eyes open, you'll want to rest your gaze steadily on one point to reduce distraction.

4. Bring your attention to your breathing. At the beginning of the practice, simply notice the air moving in and out of your body.

5. After several breaths, begin to take notice of the feeling of your breath as it comes in through your nose or mouth, travels down your neck, and moves into your lungs. Notice the expansion of your lungs as the air enters. Notice the feeling of pressure just before you exhale.

6. Attend to your breath as you exhale. Feel your muscles relax as the air moves out of your lungs. Notice the feeling of the air moving through your throat and out your nose or mouth. Take note of that brief moment just between the end of one exhale and the beginning of an inhale.

7. As you take notice of your breath, it may naturally deepen. This is okay. Don't try to control your breath or change its tempo. If it is becoming very deep and you are feeling light-headed, stop the practice and breathe normally for several breaths.

8. If your attention has wandered and you notice at any point that your thoughts are not on your breathing, simply observe to yourself that you have become distracted and return your focus to the physical sensation of breathing. Even longtime mindfulness practitioners become distracted. When you are beginning, you may find that you're distracted more often than you are focused. This is okay. Much of the practice is about learning to notice when your mind has wandered and to then bring attention back.

9. After your timer goes off or you have completed the exercise, remember to take a minute to observe how the exercise went for

you. Briefly make a note in your journal or on a blank piece of paper about your ability to focus during the exercise and any distractions that pulled you out of it. It's not necessary to write more than a few word, such as "Worry thoughts," "Planning for tomorrow's meeting," "Caught up in emotion," "Thoughts that 'This doesn't work'," or "Observed distraction several times and returned attention to breathing."

Breathing is an ideal focal point because it is always with you. As you become proficient at bringing your attention to your breath, you will be able to use it to focus your thoughts and center yourself in your everyday life. You can focus on your breathing at any time, such as while standing in line, walking, or listening to someone. It generally has a calming effect and can help collect scattered thinking.

PRACTICE: BEING PRESENT WITH THE BODY IN THREE POSITIONS

This is a mindfulness exercise to help you bring awareness to your body and recognize the connection between your body, mind, and emotions. By mindfully putting your body into different postures, you can experience the feelings, sensations, and breath of that posture.

Your body posture both expresses and influences your feelings. Changing your bearing by altering a body position can affect your attitude, your overall posture, and how you feel.

This exercise involves putting yourself in three different body postures and observing your physical sensations, thoughts, and feelings associated with that posture. After you've practiced it over the course of a few days or a week, you can transition to observing your physical sensations, thoughts, and feelings associated with any one posture of your choice. For the three different postures, you can set your timer separately for each individual posture, taking two to three minutes for each.

1. If you choose to set a timer, do so at this point.

2. Assume the first body posture by making a strong fist with each hand. Clench it tightly. Clench your teeth and tighten the muscles

of your face. While in this posture, notice the energy associated with it. Remain in this pose for two to three minutes.

    a.   Notice the muscles required to make the posture.

    b.   Take a moment to focus on different regions of your body (e.g., head, neck and shoulders, arms, torso, legs).

    c.   Notice any sensations or pain that you are experiencing.

    d.   Bring your attention to your thoughts. Allow yourself to watch your thoughts as they come and go. Do the same with emotions. If your attention wanders, simply observe that you've become distracted and return your focus to your body position.

3.   Take a moment to shake your hands and loosen your body.

4.   Assume the second body posture by relaxing your face, opening your fists, and putting your hands together and arranging your body as if in prayer. Remain in this pose for two to three minutes, bringing your attention to the same aspects as in step 1.

5.   Take a moment to shake your hands and loosen your body.

6.   Assume the third body posture by standing up straight and tall, with your feet shoulder-width apart and your arms hanging down at your sides. Keep your shoulders down or relaxed and your neck long. Remain in this pose for two to three minutes, bringing your attention to the same aspects as in step 1.

7.   Take a moment to shake your hands and loosen your body.

8.   Take a minute to observe how the exercise went for you. Did you notice differences in your body, emotions, and thoughts with the different postures? Briefly make a note in your journal or on a blank piece of paper about your ability to focus during the exercise and any distractions that pulled you out of it.

By mindfully putting your body into different postures, you can experience the feelings, sensations, and thoughts of that posture. Practice noticing the posture of your body and any corresponding thoughts, emotions, or physical sensations; it's a great way to connect to the present and gain a greater awareness of your internal experiences in any moment.

Attending to Your Experience of the World

When you're overwhelmed, you may find that your mind is not fully aware of what your body is doing and perceiving. At these times you might tend to break or spill things out of carelessness, drive without noticing how you got from one place to another, or rush through activities.

The exercise in this section will help you reconnect your mind to what you are physically experiencing. As with the previous exercises, the first few times you practice this one, aim for three to five minutes. After you have practiced several times, you can extend your practice time. During the exercise, use whatever method of timing works for you. If you set a timer, do so right before you begin the exercise. For this exercise you will need a cracker (or some other food item).

PRACTICE: FOCUSING ON EATING A CRACKER

1. With your cracker in your hand or on a plate or napkin in front of you, get settled in a comfortable sitting position. You can sit in a comfortable chair or on the floor with your legs crossed.

2. Either focus your gaze on the cracker or gently close your eyes. If you keep your eyes closed, you'll want to have the cracker in your hand so you don't need to fumble for it during the exercise.

3. Bring your attention to the cracker. Slowly put the cracker in your mouth and take a bite of it. Begin by noticing the taste and texture of the cracker. Is it salty or crunchy? You may have had expectations of what the cracker would taste like. As you slowly chew on the cracker, notice what it actually tastes like.

4. Notice any physical responses to the cracker. Does your mouth fill with saliva? Does your stomach rumble? Attend to what is happening to your body physically.

5. Now notice your evaluation of the cracker. Is its taste pleasing, bland, or displeasing? Your likes and dislikes are your judgments

about the cracker. You can notice that they are there and then bring your focus back to the act of eating the cracker.

6. Food and the act of eating can be an emotional experience for many people. Allow yourself to become aware of any emotional reaction you are having to eating the cracker or feelings that arise while you're eating the cracker. If you find you are getting caught up in your feelings, notice that and return your focus to the physical sensations of eating.

7. After your timer goes off or you have completed the exercise, remember to take a minute to observe how the exercise went for you. Briefly write a sentence or a few words about your ability to focus during the exercise and note any distractions that pulled you out of it.

As you become more mindful, your awareness of the physical, mental, and emotional experiences you are having in each moment increases. Eating is one of the many activities that people often do mindlessly. Learning to attend to this or any routine activity with mindfulness can help you begin to connect to all aspects of your life and spend less time on automatic pilot.

Labeling Your Experience

In this exercise you are going to listen to a piece of music with your full attention. The first few times you practice this exercise, it will help to have a piece of music that you feel connected to emotionally (for example, you may respond to the lyrics or sentiment or connect to a past experience you've had with the music).

PRACTICE: DESCRIBING AN EXPERIENCE WITH MUSIC

In this exercise, you will focus on putting words to your experience. The exercise instructs you to describe different aspects of the music and your experience of it. You can do this in your head, aloud softly to yourself, or in your journal or on a piece of paper.

1. If you choose to set a timer, do so at this point and start your music.

2. Begin by getting settled in a comfortable sitting position. As with the previous exercises, you can sit in a comfortable chair or on the floor with your legs crossed.

3. Either gently close your eyes or find a point in front of you on which to focus your gaze. If you keep your eyes open, you'll want to keep a steady gaze on this one point to reduce distraction.

4. Listen to the music and describe its characteristics to yourself. You can start with its genre (for example, country, pop, or classical). Now pay attention to and describe the sound of the instruments; if there is a singer, the tone of the singer's voice; the beat; the energy; and the mood of the song.

5. Notice your physical reaction to the music. Does it make you want to do things like get up and dance, jump up and down, or lie down and relax? Does your body feel like moving or staying still? Try to put words to and label the effect the music has on your body.

6. Allow yourself to become aware of any emotional reaction you are having to the music and describe that reaction. Try to label the emotion or emotions that you are experiencing. Describe to yourself any elements of the music that trigger an emotional response.

7. Tune in to any thoughts you are having. Label those thoughts. Maybe they are memories of a past experience or fantasies. Describe what your thoughts contain.

8. In this exercise you may get caught up in listening to the music or in the feelings or thoughts associated with the music. If your attention has wandered, simply observe that you've become distracted and return your focus. If you've noticed judgments about your ability to find words for your experience, label them in your mind as "judgments" and let them pass. If you get lost in judgments, bring your mind back to the music.

9. After your timer goes off or your song has ended, remember to take a minute to observe how the exercise went for you. Briefly write a sentence or a few words about your ability to focus during the exercise and any distractions that pulled you out of it.

You can bring this exercise into an array of everyday circumstances—while listening to a group conversation or while in a meeting at work, for example. The ability to describe and label your thoughts, emotions, and experiences helps you make sense of them and can decrease emotional reactivity. *Neural fMRI* (functional magnetic resonance imaging; used to see changing blood flow in the brain associated with neural activity) suggests that labeling enhances the brain's regulation of emotion and decreases painful emotions such as anger, anxiety, and fear (Creswell et al. 2007). Stress is heightened when you feel out of control and overwhelmed. Simply putting words to an experience can increase your self-efficacy and decrease intense emotions that can be overpowering and add to your burden of stress.

Mindfulness in Everyday Life

Mindfulness is taught as a way of being rather than as a technique for achieving a goal. As a way of being, it is intended to become part of your everyday life. The intentional mindfulness practices in this chapter serve as a foundation for integrating mindfulness practice into your day-to-day life. For many, the heightened emotions and physical symptoms caused by stress interfere with their ability to relax, relate to others, and let go of unhealthy coping mechanisms and habits. The following are suggestions for incorporating a greater mindful awareness into areas of your everyday life that might be suffering as a result of stress. You can use these strategies to become more aware of times of tension and stress and to improve coping.

Changing Habits That Hurt You

To change habitual actions and reactions, you must learn to pay attention to what is happening around and inside of you. Mindfulness teaches you to notice and label your own behavior, thoughts, and emotions, which is necessary when learning any new behavior or changing old habits.

Here are some mindfulness suggestions to help change habitual patterns of behavior:

- *Incorporate "mini-mindfulness" meditations* (lasting about two to five minutes each) *into your day* (consider doing this kind of meditation about every ninety minutes).

- *Practice brief breathing exercises.* Attend to routine activities with mindfulness. In these moments, notice your feelings, thoughts, and behaviors.

- *Bring your attention to your body positions several times throughout the day.* Notice how you're holding your body and the feelings associated with that position. It's not necessary to try to change your body or emotions; just bring a greater awareness to them.

- *Practice bringing your thoughts and attention to your actions.* If you are walking, be conscious that you are walking. If you are sitting, be conscious that you are sitting. Be aware of emotions and thoughts that distract you from your current activity and bring your mind back to being conscious of what you are doing in the moment.

- *During the day, when a feeling arises, notice it.*

- *Think of your emotions as a wave in the ocean* (Linehan 1993b). Don't try to get rid of them and don't engage with them. Acknowledge and recognize your emotions and notice them as they pass out of your mind. Notice how they are sometimes overwhelming, and at other times they recede, like a wave, with no need for action from you.

- *Practice observing your impulses to act* (say, to eat unhealthy snacks) *and notice how the urges come and go with time.* Don't try to fight the urge; just notice how the strength of the urge ebbs and flows throughout your day.

Work

Mindfulness can improve your work environment in a variety of ways. Bringing mindfulness into a job can help with stress-related work pressures, such as a preoccupation with failure, excessive worry about unexpected events, pressure to complete multiple tasks at once, and rigid reactions to problems.

For many, the work environment requires a very specific set of highly developed skills. Applying nonevaluative sustained attention to your work can improve your ability to master skills and complete tasks, which can lower work stress, reduce burnout, and allow you to more effectively respond to work problems.

Here are some suggestions for mindfulness at work:

- *Structure your day to decrease the amount of switching you do between tasks.* This may mean setting aside blocks of time to check e-mail rather than responding to each e-mail as it comes in, taking and returning calls at specific times, or blocking off time to complete one task before you begin another.

- *Practice mindful breathing to improve your focus and attention before answering the phone or going into a meeting.* Turn off distracting devices, such as cell phones and laptops, and focus your entire attention on the meeting or call.

- *Be conscious of interruptions throughout the day and practice making choices to stay focused on your original task or to allow yourself to shift your full attention from your original task to the source of the interruption.*

- *Schedule times for mini-mindfulness breaks, in which you focus on your breathing or attend to your body sensations and feelings.* Use these times to calm and center yourself before returning to your work.

- *At the end of the workday, take five minutes to reflect on your day and note where distractions and interruptions pulled you away from high-priority tasks.* Use this information about what is distracting you from completing important work to make changes to reduce those distractions and interruptions.

- *Notice when daily work hassles interfere with your goals and trigger intense emotions.* Practice activating wise mind by tuning in to emotional urges to act—for instance, urges to make impulsive decisions, make automatic judgments, or respond defensively. Focus on letting go of excessive emotion and doing what will work in the situation, which could include changing tactics or avoiding needless conflict.

Sleep

Worry-filled thoughts and rumination are typical features of the stress response that can contribute to sleep problems. There is evidence that increased practice of mindfulness is associated with improved sleep and the reduction of sleep-interfering stress symptoms, such as worry (Winbush, Gross, and Kreitzer 2007).

Here are some mindfulness practices to help improve sleep:

- *Expand your awareness of other factors during the day that may affect your ability to sleep.* Set aside two or three times during the day to do a mini-mindfulness practice.

- *Attend to distractions such as physical pain, muscle tension, eating habits, and exercise needs, all of which may interfere with sleep.*

- *Bring mindful attention to your routines before sleep.* Often sleep distur-bance is a result of poor sleep habits—for example, watching TV in bed, eating a heavy meal close to bedtime, bringing your computer into bed, and using your bed as an office. These are overstimulating late-night activities that disrupt sleep.

- *Over the course of a few nights, attend to the content of the worry thoughts that interfere with your sleep.* For many, nighttime worrying involves anticipating problems and planning for the next day. If you dis-cover while you're attending to your thoughts that this is the case for you, it may help to set aside time earlier in the day to focus entirely on planning. Take ten to fifteen minutes at an earlier time of day—say, early evening—and focus your full attention on anticipating potential stressors and planning for the following day's activities. At the end of your planning time, you can write down any actions that you will need to take in the morning or during the course of the next day. After your planning time, notice worry thoughts as they arise and allow yourself to let them pass.

- *Practice mindful breathing before sleep.*

- *Bring your awareness to your body and any built-up tensions from the day.*

- *Focus on relaxing your muscles in the different regions of your body.*

In Relationships

Mindfulness skills can foster greater awareness, connectedness, and acceptance in interpersonal relationships. Boosting your own stress-coping skills will improve the quality of your relationships.

Here are some suggestions for mindfulness in relationships:

- *Before important interactions, practice mindful breathing and awareness of your body position, thoughts, and emotions.*

- *Focus all your attention on listening to the other person without getting caught up in your own thoughts or emotional reactions to what they are saying.*

- *Act with wise mind.* For example, attend to everyday stressors (such as broken appliances or traffic) that cause intense emotional reactions. Notice whether those emotions make you more likely to act impulsively with others in ways that you might later regret—say, by yelling, blaming, or insulting someone.

- *Fully engage in the activity of the moment with the people in your life.* Throw yourself into being with others in both your actions and your thoughts. Put away distractions such as cell phones and other electronic gadgets. Bring your thoughts back to the current activity if you notice your mind has wandered into worries or other thoughts.

- *Focus attention on having empathy and appreciation for other people's problems or struggles.*

- *Focus on the joyful aspects of interacting with another person.*

- *Notice the contributions others make to your life.*

Wrap-Up

The practice of mindfulness can help mitigate the impact of stress on your mental and physical well-being as well as on other aspects of your life, such as problematic habits, your ability to sleep, your job performance, and your relationships. Mindfulness practice can increase your awareness of your feelings, allowing you to have thoughts and feelings that come and go without worry or rumination. This chapter highlighted the qualities of attention that are a part of the practice of mindfulness and focused on exercises aimed at incorporating mindfulness into your everyday life. This practice of mindfulness can help you focus your thoughts, increase your ability to notice and respond to the physical sensations of stress, and act with intention rather than automatically or out of habit.

CHAPTER 7

Decreasing Emotional Suffering

Stress is a part of life for everyone. Even if you make radical life changes, you cannot completely eliminate stress from your life.

However, in DBT you learn that you can offset stress and painful, stress-related emotions by creating more positive experiences and positive emotions in your life (Linehan 1993b). The focus of this chapter is on decreasing extreme stress by increasing joy, simply letting go of stress and stress-related emotions, and decreasing your vulnerability to stress by managing your lifestyle.

Increase Joy

Many people feel at the mercy of their circumstances. When life is stressful, they become stuck in a cycle of stressful events and overwhelming, stress-related emotions. Regularly experiencing conflict and pressure leaves you regularly experiencing emotions such as anger, frustration, and anxiety as well.

To decrease the amount of stress you experience and increase the joy and pleasure in your life, it helps to understand something about how they occur in the brain. Stress and joy may seem like polar opposites, but they are actually quite closely linked in the brain. *Dopamine*—a chemical substance that transmits nerve impulses across synapses in the brain—plays an important role in the experience of pleasure. And, interestingly, it is also associated with an acute stress response.

Although it may seem counterintuitive, stress hormones trigger the release of dopamine from pleasure pathways in the brain. This means that at some level, stress triggers a pleasurable response.

How can stress, which can be debilitating and leave you in anguish, be linked to the experience of pleasure? When you experience a moderate rise in stress hormones—for instance, if you see that you have received an e-mail from a prospective employer after an interview that you thought went well, you might feel a degree of stress but also anticipatory pleasure in the hope that the e-mail has positive news. When the stress is relatively short-lived, as in this case where you have only to open the e-mail, the greatest amounts of dopamine are released in the brain. Because of the release of dopamine, you might experience that particular stressful event as exciting or exhilarating rather than agonizing (Sapolsky 2004).

On the other hand, severe and prolonged stress—waiting weeks or months to hear back about a prospective job, for example—will deplete your dopamine reserves, leaving you less able to experience pleasure and happiness. Brief and moderate stress can give you a burst of energy and make you feel excited. Prolonged stress can leave you sad or depressed.

The strength of the pleasure pathways in the brain is variable, with the effect becoming stronger with more use. Like a footpath in the woods that becomes easier to travel the more it is used, these neural pathways become easier for neurotransmitters, in this case dopamine, to travel with increased use.

When you generate situations that elicit feelings of joy and happiness, you strengthen the pathways in the brain associated with the experience of pleasure. You can actively bring positive events into your life and, with time, can increase the ease with which you experience pleasure.

To increase your experience of pleasure, DBT strategies suggest that you do what you love, set and make progress toward goals, connect with others, think positive thoughts, and let go of your worries (Linehan 1993b).

Do What You Love

Don't underestimate the power a few immediate positive experiences will have on your stress levels. Activities that you love can be relaxing, satisfying, exhilarating, or exciting. Dopamine released in the brain during exhilarating activities, such as riding a roller coaster, jumping on a trampoline, or ice-skating, can make you feel excited or happy. Bowling, watching a sunset, and decorating the house with flowers are examples of activities that can be satisfying and enjoyable.

Here are some suggestions for doing what you love:

- *To strengthen pleasure pathways in the brain, schedule at least one thing a day that makes you feel good.* This might include calling a friend, listening to music, exercising, eating chocolate or food you love, lighting candles, watching a movie, taking a walk, reading a book or magazine, or being alone.

- *Plan pleasurable activities as rewards that you can anticipate.* For example, plan celebrations for hard work and accomplishments along the way.

- *If you haven't felt real joy in a while, think back to moments in your life that you found thrilling and exhilarating.* You may have to think all the way back to childhood to identify those moments. Schedule and commit to doing at least one of those thrilling or exhilarating activities.

Set Goals

Pleasure comes from the anticipation of a reward and from expectation, confidence, and a sense of mastery. Changes in levels of dopamine in the brain can occur with the simple act of anticipating and working toward a positive goal. When you anticipate that your hard work will be rewarded, you can experience pleasure in both the anticipation and the accomplishment of the task (Sapolsky 2004).

Here are some suggestions for setting goals that increase pleasure and joy and decrease stress:

- *Identify your goals.* Identify the goals that will make your life better and that, when you achieve them, will bring positive experiences into your life.

- *Set long-term positive outcomes.* Make sure achieving your goal will bring long-term positive outcomes, such as a better standard of living, better health, or closer relationships with others.

- *Set yourself up for success.* All goals include an element of loss of control because you never really know for sure whether you will be able to achieve them. Goals that you are more likely to achieve—and therefore that involve less uncertainty—are more likely to increase your sense of happiness rather than leave you feeling stressed by the pressure to achieve your goal. For instance, if your goal is to make a career change, you can get advice and guidance from career counselors and experts in the field you want to pursue, to decrease uncertainty and increase your chances of success.

- *Make short-term changes that will bring long-term results.* Pleasurable lack of control is brief, while stressful lack of control is longer term. Setting small goals that you are likely to achieve relatively quickly will keep experiences of anxiety and feelings that you can't manage the situation brief. Make daily and weekly goals that provide you with a sense of accomplishment and keep you progressing towards larger objectives. In the example of making a career change, setting achievable weekly goals for such things as networking, getting professional training, or polishing your professional documents will make short-term progress clear, which will leave you energized rather than stressed.

- *Schedule small steps into your daily life.* You are much more likely to achieve goals if you take small steps that are easily incorporated into your daily life. If your goal requires you to overhaul major aspects of your daily routines, you make it more difficult to achieve, which makes it less certain that you will achieve it. This increases the likelihood that the goal will be stressful, rather than pleasurable.

- *Continually assess your progress.* From time to time, look back at your weekly goals. Are you achieving them? And by achieving these weekly goals, are you making progress toward your larger goal? When you assess progress, you can gain pleasure from successes along the way. And if you're spinning in circles, you can reconsider how you plan to get to your goal.

Bond with Friends and Family

In chapter 5, I discussed the important role that relationships play in decreasing stress. The need to belong is a powerful and fundamental human drive, and forming strong, stable relationships has positive effects on mood (Baumeister and Leary 1995). Individual and cultural differences have an impact on exactly what, in any relationship, contributes to a sense of happiness. However, to be happy, people generally need regular, pleasant interactions with a few other people who are concerned about their welfare.

Here are some suggestions for increasing happiness through closeness with others:

- *Pay attention to friends and loved ones.* Focus on being kind, compassionate, and nonjudgmental. Listen when they're having a hard time.

- *Get interested in the activities of friends and loved ones.*

- *Express gratitude.* Expressing gratitude improves your relationships by improving the other person's positive view of you. One study suggests that this, in turn, increases a person's investment in the long-term well-being of the relationship with you. It also increases the other person's comfort in voicing relationship concerns, which is an important part of relationship well-being (Lambert and Fincham 2011).

Think Positive Thoughts

In chapter 2, I discussed the influence of your thinking on your experience of stress and the intensity of your stress-related emotions. It is your interpretation of events (for instance, viewing them as demanding and seeing problems as insurmountable) that triggers the body's stress response. Ignoring the negative aspects of difficult circumstances can result in denial and longer-term suffering. However, spending large amounts of time focused on only the difficult and negative aspects of your life can result in similar negative emotional consequences.

Negative emotions last only a few seconds, but thinking about and focusing on the things that are bothering you can keep those emotions around for much longer. If you tend to focus on the negative, make a conscious effort to refocus on the positive aspects of stressful circumstances and the positive events in your life.

Here are some suggestions for thinking positively:

- *Remember what happened today or this week that made you smile, laugh, or feel a sense of calm.*

- *Refocus on the potential positive outcomes of your circumstances.*

- *Remember that opportunity usually accompanies crisis and change.* Think about how your current circumstances might be an opportunity for positive change.

- *Take a few minutes and relive positive moments in your mind.* Allow yourself to repeat a conversation in your mind or daydream about exactly what occurred, and then reexperience the good emotions you felt.

Let Go of Worries

Worrying is one of the most common symptoms of stress. The act of worrying can increase stress levels and perpetuate the experience of stress. Each time you anticipate a future stressful event with your worrying, you trigger the body's stress response.

The mindfulness skills you learned in chapter 6 are particularly helpful for letting go of worries. You can use them to increase your awareness of when you worry and to gain control of your own mind so that you're not stuck in worry thoughts.

Here are some suggestions for letting go of worries:

- *If you notice yourself worried, first acknowledge your worry.* Then tell yourself to let it go. You might say to yourself, *That's not worth worrying about* or simply *Let it go.*

- *Refocus on the positive aspects of your life and the goals you've set for yourself.*

- *Any time you find yourself worrying, inhale and exhale slowly.* Repeat several times until your thoughts have slowed as well.

- *Look out a window, at a painting on the wall, or at anything that is relatively still.* Bring your attention to parts of your experience you usually ignore. Notice the space between your fingers. Feel your feet on the ground or your back against your chair. Engage in active mindfulness exercises that require your full attention. Try exercises such as balloon breath, walking with a mantra, or the air exercise (all in chapter 3). Throw yourself completely into the activity of the moment. Whatever you are doing, do it with your full attention.

Let Go of Stress

When you're stressed, it's easy to become caught up in painful emotions triggered by stressful circumstances. You might feel rejected and spiral into loneliness and despair or feel slighted and become stuck in thoughts of anger and retaliation.

To get out of a cycle of intense negative emotions, it's sometimes most effective to simply focus on letting these emotions go. To let go of stress-related emotions, you need to first allow yourself to be present with them.

PRACTICE: LETTING GO OF PAINFUL EMOTIONS

The purpose of this exercise is to acknowledge and allow unpleasant feelings—such as anger, anxiety, and fear that are often a part of the stress response—to pass. Instead of being trapped in a cycle of intense emotion, in this exercise you will recognize and sit with your internal experience of an unpleasant feeling and then let it go.

1. Find a quiet time when you are unlikely to be distracted for five to ten minutes. Sit quietly and bring your attention toward your feelings. Notice the emotion that you're stuck in.

2. Watch your emotion. Action is not necessary. Internally experience both the thoughts and physical effects of your emotion.

3. Don't try to push your emotion away. Welcome your emotion. You might want to imagine it as a traveler who has come to your door. In your mind, invite the emotion to stay with you.

4. It might seem counterintuitive to sit with and welcome an emotion that you're trying to rid yourself of. But the act of mindfully attending to your emotion helps you to create some distance. It allows you to be with your emotion without reacting to it.

5. Name your emotion. Notice the emotion that you're stuck in and name it. For example, you might say to yourself, *I'm feeling angry or enraged or afraid.* Recognizing the physical and mental experience of the emotion may help you find a name for what you are feeling. If you're having trouble finding a name for your feeling, it may help to look at the Related Emotions table in chapter 1.

6. Appreciate your emotion. Think of your emotions as helpers that inform you about your world and help motivate you to do what you need to do. As you breathe, imagine your emotions helping you make sense of the world around you and your internal experiences. Attend to your feeling and say to yourself, *Breathing in, I am grateful for my anger* (or whatever emotion you're experiencing) and *Breathing out, I value its help.*

7. Focus on letting your feelings go. Change what you're saying to yourself from *Breathing out, I value [the emotion's] help* to *Breathing out, I let my anger [or other feeling] go.* As you become aware of thoughts that activate and intensify the emotion—and the physical changes in your body that are related to the experience of the emotion—acknowledge them and let them pass without actively engaging in the thoughts or responding to your physical experience.

8. Allow your emotion to pass. Observe how, over time, one emotion passes and another occurs. Let go of the thoughts and actions that would once more set off your unpleasant feeling. Acknowledge that you have had the feeling. Acknowledge thoughts and physical reactions related to the feeling and allow them to pass. You might say to yourself, *I recognize angry thoughts* or *The tension in my jaw is related to the feeling of anger.* Let the thoughts and feelings pass without engaging with them.

This last step might take several repetitions and only come to you over the course of time.

By recognizing your feelings and staying with them rather than suppressing or pushing them away, you can begin to transform them. As you acknowledge and accept them as a part of life without reacting to them, you will find that you are no longer stuck in or controlled by those emotions. Instead, you will be able to let them go.

Decrease Your Vulnerability to Stress

To bring greater happiness into your life and decrease the impact of stressful circumstances on your ability to function, it's critical to attend to daily habits. Everyday activities and routines can either increase or decrease the amount and intensity of stress that you experience. Over time you can fall into patterns that exacerbate stress and leave you emotionally reactive, or you can live a lifestyle that improves your ability to cope with stressful circumstances.

Habits and routines in your everyday life can make you more vulnerable to stress. In the short run, that bag of chips or late-night TV show may feel like a stress reliever. But long-term, these things may actually cause additional stress. This section focuses on specific activities identified in DBT that are part of your life and that you can better manage in order to decrease your vulnerability to intense emotion (Linehan 1993b).

Get Adequate Sleep

Why do we sleep? Eating, breathing, and sleeping are basic human drives. Despite our twenty-four-hour culture, we are unable to forego sleep. Sleep plays a role in encoding and assimilating memories, integrating new information, maintaining cognitive functioning, and modulating and regulating emotional arousal. It prevents us from wasting energy and provides a period of restoration during which wear and tear on the body and brain is repaired.

Disturbed sleep can have a significant impact on your quality of life. It can negatively impact physical performance, impair work performance, disrupt social functioning, and increase emotional reactivity, irrationality, irritability, and lethargy.

Adequate restful sleep is critical to good health. Insufficient restful sleep can result in mental and physical health problems and increase sympathetic nervous system activity, which mobilizes the body's stress response and can induce the fight-or-flight response.

Sleep disturbances also contribute to the stressful demands you encounter (for example, what you experience in the aftermath of poor work performance or during periods of increased problems in a relationship). Additionally, problems with sleep contribute to the intensity of stress-related painful emotions.

Sleep disturbances not only negatively impact stress—stress interferes with sleep. After extreme situational stress, people tend to have more wakeful episodes and increased movements that disturb sleep. Insomnia (which is characterized by the perception that you don't get enough sleep and that you can't fall asleep, stay asleep, or get back to sleep once you've awakened during the night) is commonly experienced during times of stress. Typically insomnia lasts for a night or two, but it can go on for weeks, months, or even years.

Here are some suggestions for sleep habits that can lower stress:

- *Keep regular sleep hours.* The average adult needs 7.5 to 8.5 hours of sleep a night. This is particularly important for people who do shift work, which requires them to be up overnight. The human body's biological clock, which programs us to feel sleepy during the nighttime hours and to be active during the daylight hours, puts people who work the night shift at risk for sleep disturbance and, as a result, increased stress.

- *Exercise regularly,* but not late in the day or close to bedtime.

- *Get natural light exposure.*

- *Limit caffeine,* particularly within six hours of sleep.

- *Avoid nicotine.*

- *Avoid naps,* especially after 3:00 p.m.

- *Early in the evening, plan for the next day and then allow yourself time to let go of worries before bed.* Try not to worry about whether or not you will be able to sleep.

- *If you drink alcohol, do so in moderation.*

- *Develop a bedtime ritual.* For instance, you might read, listen to music, take a hot bath or do relaxation exercises before you turn out all the lights. If you can't sleep after twenty minutes, go to another room and engage in a quiet activity until you feel drowsy.

- *Don't over- or undereat before bed.*

- *Sleep in comfortable conditions.* Keep the room at a comfortable temperature, use soft bedding, reduce noise as much as possible, and get rid of distractions such as TV and computers.

- *Be aware of factors that may impact sleep:* menopause, menstrual cycle, pregnancy and childbirth, work requirements, pain and illness, body aches, and a need to use the bathroom.

- *Get a diagnosis.* Because insomnia can become a chronic problem, it is important to get it diagnosed and treated if it persists for more than a month. If you consistently have trouble sleeping, see a doctor to determine whether underlying health issues could be contributing to problems with sleep.

Exercise

If you exercise regularly, the physical and mental health benefits may be clear and readily apparent to you. Exercise triggers the release of *endorphins*, natural chemicals in the body that produce a feeling of well-being. But many people struggle to incorporate a regular routine that includes physical activity into their lives, so they miss out on this important stress reducer.

Exercise improves both mental and physical responses to stress. It enhances your ability to cope with stress and produces a long-term resilience to stressors (Salmon 2001). With exercise, mood generally improves, and evidence suggests that exercise reduces symptoms of anxiety and can improve self-perceptions and self-esteem (Fox 1999). Exercise can be a diversion from stressors, provide a sense of mastery, and reduce muscle tension.

Exercise releases some of the energy of an acute stress response, particularly when you experience psychological stress and don't release energy through a physical response to the stressor. Aerobic exercise protects against the harmful physical consequences of chronic stress by lowering blood pressure and resting heart rate and increasing lung capacity. Exercise has a positive impact on stress-related diseases such as coronary heart disease, diabetes, and obesity. People who are aerobically fit have a reduced response to psychosocial stressors such as the breakup of a relationship or the pressure of an upcoming work deadline (Crews and Landers 1987).

Here are some ways to use exercise to lower stress:

- *Consider what type of exercise you prefer to do.* You are more likely to actually engage in exercise that you like, and enjoyable exercise is more likely to promote well-being than to be perceived as an increased pressure or demand.

- *Exercising during the working day has a positive impact on mood.* Try to fit an active break into your workday, particularly if you work in a sedentary environment.

- *Exercise on a regular basis.* To have an impact on your stress response, you need to exercise for a minimum of twenty to thirty minutes, a few times a week (Sapolsky 2004).

- *Incorporate even brief sessions of exercise into your day.* Brief, intense aerobic exercise can induce modest reductions in temporary anxiety, while thirty minutes of aerobic exercising—say, running—can reduce negative mood.

- *Don't overexercise.* Too much of anything, including exercise, can exacerbate rather than decrease stress.

Treat Illness and Pain

In chapter 1, I discussed the role that stress can play in the development of physical health problems. For instance, stress has adverse effects on hypertension and coronary heart disease as well as a role in the development of a host of other health problems such as obesity and diabetes.

Even shorter-term, acute stress can have an impact on physical health. In a study investigating the impact of daily stress on health, Anita DeLongis and colleagues found a significant relationship between daily stress and the occurrence of health problems such as flu, sore throat, headaches, and backaches (DeLongis, Lazarus, and Folkman 1988).

Just as stress has an impact on the functioning of the body, the functioning of the body has an impact on your levels of stress. If you view the body as a whole system, you can see that it is not possible to isolate your physical health from your mental functioning.

Illness, whether it comes in the form of cancer or the flu, can induce worry, fear, and anxiety. Illness and pain create an increased stress burden; contributing factors may include doctor's visits, loss of control over your body, indignities in the health care system, side effects of medications, uncertainty of medical outcomes, physical limitations of illness, expense of medical care, and lost work.

Here are some health strategies that can help lower stress:

- *Be an active participant in your own health care.* Actively participating in your own health care can increase your sense of control and decrease worry and fear.

- *Learn more about your health and how to maintain it.*

- *Learn to communicate effectively with doctors and health care providers.* Make sure that you are understood and, conversely, that you understand the professionals involved in your health care.

- *Recognize that your body, mind, emotions, and stress levels are interconnected.*

- *Attend to how your lifestyle and other environmental factors influence your health.*

- *Attend to your thoughts and attitudes about your health.* Seeing your health problems as a challenge and attempting to exert meaningful control over your circumstances may increase your ability to cope with the stress of illness and pain.

- *View the symptoms of your illness or health problems as messages from your body.* Rather than immediately trying to get rid of them, listen to them to better understand and respond to your physical problems.

Eating and Nutrition

Stress and eating are intimately and reciprocally connected. The experience of stress can impact your appetite and eating habits. At the same time, your eating habits can exacerbate stress-related health issues.

For some people, stress is associated with increased eating and, in particular, increased consumption of sweet and high-fat foods. For others, stress is associated with a lack of appetite and restricted food intake.

It is unclear why some people respond to stress with increased eating while others respond by restricting their eating. Individual differences in learning, attitudes, and biology are all likely to impact how you eat when under stress. However, emotional and physiological changes that occur in response to stress also appear to have an impact on eating. In one study, both negative mood associated with stress and the physiological aspects of the stress response in the form of high cortisol levels (*cortisol* is a hormone secreted during the stress response and is responsible for many of the stress-related changes in the body) were significantly related to greater food consumption (Epal et al. 2001). In fact, under chronic stress, the finely balanced system that regulates the body's intake and consumption of energy may become unregulated, possibly contributing to overeating (Adam and Epal 2007).

Over time, stress-related overeating can impact weight and health. In extreme cases these eating behaviors can lead to obesity and bulimic episodes. The practice of restrained eating also has health risks beyond the mood instability and irritability that come with hunger. Anorexia nervosa is the most devastating effect of continual restrained eating.

As I discussed earlier in this book, chronic stress has an impact on your health. It increases your risk of developing certain diseases, such as cardiovascular disease and diabetes. Nutrition and eating can play a significant role in the management of some of these stress-related health problems.

Here are some ways that eating habits can help lower stress:

There is no one "right" way to eat. However, there are some basic principles that will keep your eating healthy and balanced, reducing your vulnerability to stress.

- *According to the American Dietetic Association, calories play a critical role in balanced eating.* For a balanced diet, begin by getting the recommended amount of calories each day for your gender, weight, activity level, and age.

- *Eat nutritionally rich foods.* Fresh fruits, vegetables, whole grains, and lean proteins provide your body with essential nutrients that it needs to function.

- *Eat throughout the day.* Don't skip meals or restrict food and then get all your calories at one time. Eating throughout the day keeps your body fueled, which improves energy and reduces mood fluctuations. Increase your awareness of your eating style.

- *Avoid overeating.* Both *restrained eaters*—people who are conscious of trying to restrict the amount of food that they eat in a typical meal—and *emotional eaters*—people who eat out of emotional need rather than nutritional need—are more likely to overeat when under stress.

- *If you suffer from health problems related to chronic stress, follow nutritional guidelines that may improve your health and stress symptoms.* For example, nutrients, such as the omega-3 fatty acids found in certain fishes and nuts, have beneficial effects on cardiovascular disease (Kris-Etherton, Harris, and Appel 2003).

- *Don't deprive yourself.* Comfort foods and treats can play an important role in coping with stress. Incorporate moderate amounts of foods into your diet that may be lower in nutritional value but provide psychological comfort.

Avoid Mood-Altering Drugs

It's not uncommon for people to use alcohol and other drugs to "take the edge off" when they're feeling stressed. Alcohol is the most commonly used mood-altering drug, but others include stimulants, such as nicotine and cocaine; opioids, such as heroin and oxycodone; sedatives, such as lorazepam; and hallucinogens, such as marijuana. Mood-altering drugs can be illegal, prescribed, or over-the-counter drugs.

THE INTERACTIONS BETWEEN MOOD-ALTERING DRUGS AND STRESS

Drugs that impact mood are diverse, and the effects of these drugs on the body and the brain are varied. However, some consistent characteristics are that they make you feel less stressed, at least momentarily, and they all play a role in the release of dopamine, the neurotransmitter discussed earlier in the chapter that is involved in the experience of pleasure. The activation of those pleasure pathways makes you more likely to return to the drug again and again to get a break from stress. In fact, the anticipation of the pleasure can keep you coming back despite negative life consequences. In addition to activating the release of dopamine, these drugs are also all addictive. With addictive properties come tolerance and habituation. Unlike pleasurable life experiences—say, listening to a favorite song—which strengthen pleasure pathways in the brain, mood-altering drugs flood synapses with dopamine, causing the neurons to compensate by becoming less sensitive. What this means is that with continued use, more and more of the drug is required to create the same pleasurable experience (Sapolsky 2004).

The risk of using mood-altering drugs to manage your stress is that you transition from simply wanting a pleasurable experience to needing the drug. With decreased sensitivity to dopamine, the absence of a drug can decrease your ability to experience pleasure. You need the drug to get out of negative emotions, thus creating a cycle of extreme emotional highs and lows, with little equilibrium.

ALCOHOL AND STRESS

People tend to feel less stressed when under the influence of alcohol. It can blunt the magnitude of the physiological stress response and reduce anxiety. It can also change how you're thinking about stressors. When you're drunk, it's easy to forget those life demands that are stressing you out.

However, as the alcohol leaves your system, so do the stress-reducing effects. In fact, alcohol is in your system and reducing your stress response for a shorter period of time than when it's leaving your system and increasing your stress levels.

If you are recovering from an addiction to alcohol, stress increases your chances of a relapse, and ongoing stress increases the extent of alcohol abuse (Sapolsky 2004). People who are more sensitive and reactive to stress—those who have a vulnerability to stress—are at increased risk to become addicted to alcohol.

Wrap-Up

The techniques in this chapter are designed to help you increase the pleasure in your life, let go of painful stress-related emotions, and structure your lifestyle to reduce the impact of stressful circumstances. This chapter explored the interaction between stress and daily habits and suggested strategies to modify those routines in your everyday life that may be contributing to your stress.

CHAPTER 8

Approaching, Not Avoiding

The relationship between life stressors and emotions operates in two directions. Life stressors typically increase your experience of painful emotions; at the same time, how you respond to and cope with your experience of painful emotions makes a significant difference in whether your behavior results in additional stressful life events.

Certain emotional responses to life stressors can make you want to avoid those stressors. Fear, anxiety, and shame are intense stress-related emotions that can narrow your thinking and leave you feeling isolated and out of control, generating an urge to escape.

A certain amount of avoidance is normal. Most people experience episodes of avoidance in response to stressful life events. Chapter 4 even teaches strategies to get through a moment of crisis that include distracting and distancing yourself from immediate painful emotions and thoughts.

However, *avoidance* is a coping style that can lead to additional life stressors when avoiding things that upset you becomes a longer-term coping style. When you avoid rather than approach stressful circumstances, you prevent yourself from processing and understanding stressful events that impact your life.

Not only does avoidance interfere with your ability to process stress-related situations, it also interferes with your ability to solve the real problems that contribute to stressful life circumstances. Problems increase with avoidance. For example, financial and health issues may worsen when they are avoided rather than addressed, and interpersonal relationships may deteriorate with the increased strain that can come when people avoid conflict and disagreements. When these problems that contribute to stress go unresolved, they grow.

Clinical syndromes such as *agoraphobia*—where a person avoids all situations in which they don't feel safe, including contact with the outside world—severely limits life experiences. And *social phobia*—where a person avoids social contact—is another example of a disorder associated with behaviors developed to avoid experiencing fear and anxiety. The avoidance that is central to these two syndromes has a major effect on the quality of life.

Using avoidance to cope leaves problems unresolved, which contributes to increased problems and restricts life experiences.

Avoidance Can Be Counterproductive

Avoidance of physical threats is adaptive. When fear is a direct result of a physical threat—say an out-of-control vehicle or a sudden drop in an elevator—the urge to "get out of here" and avoid both the feeling of fear and the situation is adaptive. The feelings and behavioral urges associated with direct physical threats are considered *true alarms*.

But when you are reacting to a psychological threat or when your perception of the danger you face is flawed, your *avoidance urge* (the inclination to keep away from certain situations, people, feelings, or objects) may be counterproductive. Painful emotions such as anxiety and shame can be experienced even when there is little or no threat in the environment. Worry thoughts with flawed perceptions of danger and risk such as *I can't deal with it* and *These problems could happen again* contribute to the intensity of anxiety and the urge to avoid problems and circumstances that are associated with feeling anxious.

- *False alarms.* Feelings of apprehension or impending doom or distressing physical sensations (such as pounding heart and sweating) can cause you to avoid situations in which there is no risk of physical harm.

- *Psychological threats.* Fear of losing important goals, such as a relationship or a job, can cause you to avoid dealing with important problems.

- *Learned anxiety.* Memories of past anxiety that is easily recalled may be so vivid and intense that you avoid any associations with past-anxiety–provoking situations. Stress can intensify the experience of an emotion and increase your urge to avoid any contact with painful stress-related emotional cues.

Although these perceptions are painful, remember that avoiding emotional experiences ensures that your experiences will continue to trigger painful emotions. Coping through behavioral avoidance is not associated with changes in feelings of depression or anxiety. If you don't want to exacerbate your problems, you must stop avoiding the experiences associated with false alarms, psychological threats, and learned anxiety.

Understanding the Task of Approaching

Stepping outside your comfort zone and experiencing fear, apprehension, anger, and guilt is one of the primary ways to reduce needless anxiety about an experience. In the case of learned anxiety, exposing yourself to the stressful situation or stress-related emotion without negative consequences teaches you that a past threat no longer exists. Approaching a feared psychological threat—for instance, dealing with financial problems you've previously avoided—can teach you that, although painful, the circumstances won't kill you. In the case of avoiding dealing with finances, faulty beliefs that *I can't handle my finances* or *If I look at my debt, it will be disastrous* won't change unless you approach your financial circumstances and learn that you can handle them and it's not disastrous.

Avoidance as a long-term coping style may be a learned response. Past experiences have an impact on whether you tend to avoid stress-related emotions. For example, a history of parental punishment, minimization of problems and parental distress when you expressed negative emotions often results in a style of avoiding stress-related emotions (Krause, Mendelson, and Lynch 2003). Over time, you may find yourself avoiding certain types of stressful situations altogether, such as social gatherings, speaking in front of work colleagues, dealing with bills or health problems, or going to the dentist.

In DBT, modified versions of *exposure-based procedures*—which involve experiencing a feared event or situation on purpose in a setting where there is no actual danger—are used to reduce painful emotions that keep you from dealing with stressful circumstances. Procedures used include exposing yourself to events that prompt these emotions but in situations you can deal with. This exposure includes *blocking* and even reversing *automatic avoidance* (Linehan 1993a). The task—approaching rather than continuing to avoid—is to confront information and events from which you have previously kept away. When you approach, you actively put yourself in stressful situations and allow yourself to think about stressful topics, such as feared outcomes, conflicts, and painful memories. The task is to enter and stay in the stressful situation in both your actions and your thoughts.

> Some people cope with stressful events in harmful and destructive ways. To work with exposure-based procedures, you'll need to be able to respond to emotional upheaval without engaging in destructive behaviors. Learning healthy strategies to deal with the stress and emotion in your life and gaining control over any high-risk behaviors, such as self-injury or suicide attempts, is an important first step *before* you consider approaching new situations that might temporarily increase your experience of painful emotions.
>
> It's advisable to wait until you have developed coping strategies and are no longer actively engaging in high-risk behaviors before trying the strategies in this chapter. If you are currently struggling with high-risk behaviors, use these strategies only with the help of a professional.

Corrective Experiences

When you interpret circumstances as threatening, but your interpretation is faulty, or when you anticipate threats that are unlikely to occur, you spend a lot of time stressed out but not in any actual danger. Fear of losing important goals can leave you feeling stressed out, but without action, the fear continues unabated and the problems remain.

The purpose of exposing yourself to stressful circumstances is to have corrective experiences. A *corrective experience* reexposes you to situations that were stressful in the past, but in a context where feared outcomes—for example, a traumatic event or your financial ruin—don't occur. The idea is that you have learned to become stressed in certain situations and that avoidance perpetuates your stress. In the example of avoiding money problems, you may have found that dealing with bills by putting them unopened into the back of a drawer temporarily decreases your stress levels. But over time, anything connected with bills may begin to trigger a stress response. Checking the mail, the sight of the mail truck, e-mails from the bank, and phone calls all might become associated with your bills and therefore can activate a stress response. In cases of trauma, cues associated with the traumatic event—for instance, the sound of a vacuum cleaner, the honk of a horn, or the smell of a shampoo—will activate the stress response before you are consciously aware of what has triggered it (Sapolsky 2004).

A corrective experience exposes you to these cues that trigger the stress response; when the feared outcome doesn't occur, you learn that the situation is not as stressful and threatening as you'd imagined and so doesn't need to be avoided. In the example of avoiding your bills, looking at how much money you owe might be distressing, but physically, you are safe. Your emotion won't kill you.

Gaining New Information

You have to put yourself in stressful circumstances and activate your stress response to acquire new information about how threatening (or not threatening) the situation is. This might mean putting yourself in a stressful situation—for instance, if you're fearful about speaking in public, you may attend a meeting in which you are expected to introduce yourself. You can also put yourself in a stressful circumstance by reading about them, watching them on TV, or imagining them.

Finding the "Right" Circumstances

Once you've decided that you want to approach situations where your stress-related emotions are unwarranted, exaggerated, or contributing to problems in your life, you need to determine when and how to begin.

When you begin to approach a stressful situation, is it better to approach slowly, dipping a toe into the shallow end of the pool and getting comfortable with that before gradually entering to your ankles and so on until you're fully immersed in stressful circumstances? Or is it better to jump into the deep end?

It turns out that both methods are related to reductions in fear and anxiety under stressful circumstances. Feelings of fear and anxiety can become less powerful after your emotion is triggered by increasingly stressful situations over a period of time or after you're flooded with intense fear all at once. For most people, *flooding* (that is, jumping into the deep end of the pool) is much more painful than gradually entering stressful situations. For example, if you're afraid to speak in public, a television appearance in front of a live audience would likely be more stressful than starting off by giving a toast at a family dinner and then slowly approaching more stressful situations.

PRACTICE: DEVELOPING A HIERARCHY OF STRESSFUL EVENTS

To get a better sense of which situations are extremely stressful to you and which trigger only a mild stress response, it helps to identify and rate stressful circumstances, creating a hierarchy of situations that include mildly to extremely stressful events.

1. Find a quiet time during the day and take out your journal or a blank piece of paper.

2. Create a table with two columns, labeling one column "Stressful Event" and the other "Intensity of Stress."

3. In the first column, write down anything that you avoid because it triggers feelings of stress.

4. In the second column, rate the level of stress you imagine you'd experience in the situation, on a scale of 1 to 5. Do you imagine it could be as bad as it ever gets? That's a 5. Would you be anxious and jittery, stuck in negative thoughts, but still functioning? Fill in a 3. Or would it be a mild nervousness that's distracting but manageable? That's a 1.

5. Put your list in order so that the lowest numbers are at the top and the highest numbers are at the bottom. You will use this hierarchy to help you decide which stressful situations to approach first. Most people prefer to begin with the lower numbers and slowly approach the more and more intensely stressful situations.

Certain characteristics of any given situation can have an impact on how stressful it is for you; for instance, if you tend to avoid dealing with your finances, unexpected bills may trigger a more intense stress response than bills you anticipated. An example of someone dealing with avoidance of financial circumstances might look like this.

Hierarchy of Stressful Financial Circumstances

Stressful Events	Intensity of Stress
Adding up everything I owe	*5*
Putting unopened bills out on the table	*3*
Calculating monthly payments necessary to reduce debt	*5*
Looking at my bank balance	*3*
Calling a financial advisor	*2*
Making lifestyle changes to reduce debt	*5*

Practice Approaching

With even brief exposure, you can become more accustomed to stressful circumstances. During the exposure, you learn that feared outcomes—say, criticism, abandonment, or death—aren't going to happen and what does happen isn't as terrible as you imagined. In stressful circumstances, your stress response initially increases, then plateaus, and finally gradually decreases. Staying in stressful situations long enough for your stress-related emotions and physical reactions to begin to decrease will reduce the intensity of future stress reactions to that type of situation. But exposure doesn't have to last that long: even brief exposures or a situation that you leave before your stress response decreases can have positive effects on your stress levels.

Imagined Stress Situations

The idea of entering stressful situations can be scary. Imagining that stressful situation can be a first step in approaching it. People respond differently to imagined stressful circumstances; some people never actually have to be in a situation to reduce the stress associated with it.

You can imagine yourself in stressful situations in a wide variety of ways: You can watch movies or plays in which the characters encounter the stressful circumstances you avoid. You can write out a description of a situation or verbally describe it to a friend or loved one. Or you can think about yourself in the stressful situation. Imagining yourself in stressful circumstances has to trigger your stress response in order to be effective. If imagining the situation doesn't increase your stress levels at least to some degree, you won't experience any reduction of stress in the real situation.

Maintaining Control

Stress is increased by the feeling that you have lost control. If you anticipate that an event will be stressful, feeling that you have little or no control over the outcome or how long you have to stay in it will only increase your feelings of stress. Although it's impossible to have complete control over any aspect of life, approaching stressful circumstances voluntarily and having a sense of control over your own behavior—how long you stay in the circumstances and how you leave them—is crucial.

Important aspects of control include feeling that you have made a choice to approach a situation and that you can influence when the experience ends. For example, if you are dealing with financial avoidance, you might choose to spend an hour collecting, opening, and organizing bills. At the end of the hour, you might then do something else or choose to distract yourself and then plan to return to your finances for another specific block of time later in the day or week.

Another important aspect of control is the ability to respond to emotional upheaval without engaging in destructive behaviors. As mentioned above, wait until you have developed coping strategies and are no longer actively engaging in high-risk behaviors before trying the strategies in this chapter.

Blocking Avoidance

If you want to feel less stress when you approach stressful circumstances, you have to block your own urge to avoid. To make it work, you have to approach the situation with both your mind and your body. Opening up bills, all the while thinking, *This is awful* and *I can't stand it* is approaching the situation only with your body. To approach with both your body and mind, you need to face your bills and think, *I can do this* and *I'm feeling shaky, but I can handle this.*

Because it's so important to block avoidance in your thoughts, you need to be committed before you begin approaching rather than avoiding stressful circumstances. If you're not sure or you don't think it's for you, you'll likely approach only part of the way, which leaves you still feeling stressed and ultimately supports your belief that you can't handle the situation.

PRACTICE: ACT DIFFERENTLY

In this exercise you will change how you act in situations that you currently avoid due to stress.

1. Choose one of the situations from the list you made in the exercise Practice: Developing a Hierarchy of Stressful Events, earlier in this chapter. If your plan is to ease yourself into this situation by exposure to increasingly stressful circumstances, begin by choosing something from the list that has a lower intensity rating.

2. Identify what you will have to do to approach the situation. If you avoid dealing with debt, you will need to open bills and look at

them. Remember that it helps to feel that you are in control of the circumstances, so try to choose something that allows you to determine how long you stay in the stressful circumstances. You may want to start by imagining approaching the situation rather than actually doing so.

3. Approach the situation in both your actions and your thoughts. This can include entering the situation, allowing yourself to notice your stress levels, and staying in the situation.

4. When you notice an urge to avoid, particularly in your thoughts, try to prevent yourself from doing so. While in the situation, be alert to anxious thoughts such as *I can't do this* or *I have to get out of here*. Practice changing your thoughts to something more manageable such as *This is hard, but I can handle it, I feel out of control, but I will survive* or *I'll muddle through*.

5. Repeat this process over and over until approaching becomes a natural response and your stress levels decrease.

6. Repeat this process with the more stressful events on your hierarchy.

Acting in a new way is hard. It's okay to be scared or apprehensive about putting yourself into situations you've previously avoided. Approaching will allow you to solve problems and deal with aspects of your life in a more productive way.

Wrap-Up

Avoidance is a coping style that can contribute to life stressors. When you avoid problems, they go unresolved and may grow. In this chapter you have learned the factors to consider when approaching situations you've previously avoided and how to act differently. These strategies will strengthen your ability to solve problems and participate fully in a wide variety of life's experiences that you previously avoided. Over time, approaching new situations will reduce your stress levels.

CHAPTER 9

Developing Trust in Yourself

Any time you make changes in your life, you create stress. Even changing to healthier coping strategies can, in the short term, trigger more stress. Developing the ability to trust, be compassionate toward, and be supportive of yourself helps balance the emotional intensity triggered by the process of change. Learning to trust your own responses and to be compassionate and supportive about those responses is an essential part of reducing your stress.

Mistrust of self is, in itself, a source of extreme stress. Self-mistrust can come from daily stresses—such as criticism, being disrespected, doing something you're not good at, or being misunderstood—or from a life event that challenges your beliefs about the world, such as loss of a job, trauma, or death.

Uncertainty as well as not knowing whom to believe—yourself or others—also produces stress and anxiety and interferes with your ability to identify the problems to be solved and the strategies that best fit your strengths and personality. When under stress, you may question your own previously held beliefs because they no longer seem relevant to your current circumstances. Uncertainty and self-mistrust also occur when people trivialize your experience, criticize your behavior, or are intolerant of your emotions.

DBT emphasizes the critical role that understanding and accepting yourself and your experiences plays in the process of change. DBT procedures include strategies to understand emotional, cognitive, and behavioral responses to life events (Linehan 1993a). The focus of this chapter is on expressing your stress-related thoughts and feelings, understanding your behaviors when under stress, and learning to be compassionate and understanding of your thoughts. You will practice seeing your stress-related reactions as understandable in the context of your life and the current moment.

Validation and Finding Self-Trust

We learn about ourselves as children through parental attention to changes in our behavior and a parent's labeling of what that behavior represents. For example, if a child is irritable, a parent might correctly or incorrectly identify any number of causes, including fatigue, hunger, difficulty mastering a new skill, or bullying at school.

Even as adults, we can gain a greater understanding of our own internal experience with correct identification of the causes of stress. A partner who correctly pinpoints an unfinished project at work as the source of your ongoing high stress levels will help you to make sense of your current frustrations and anxieties.

However, if the people around you tell you that your emotions are overblown or that you're stressed out for no reason, you're more likely to try to suppress the expression of your emotions and to doubt your own experience. With DBT, dismissal or trivialization of or punishment for the expression of your internal experience is considered *invalidating*; that is, it undermines your trust in your own emotions and understanding of your experiences (Linehan 1993a).

Validation and self-validation communicate understanding and decrease the intensity of stress-related emotions. *Validation*—the communication from others that your emotions, thoughts, or feelings are meaningful, understandable, and authentic—can help you identify your stress-related emotions, physiological stress response, and thoughts. Validation from others helps you make sense of your individual experience of stress and how the interaction between you and your current circumstances has an impact on your stress levels.

Self-validation—the ability to pay attention to and accept your own experiences, emotions, thoughts, and feelings—is equally important for developing trust in your own reactions to stressful events in your life. Self-validation is turning the light of understanding onto yourself and, given your history and current life context, viewing your own responses as authentic. Even a stress response that is out of proportion to the stressful event that triggered it can make sense if you understand your own emotional reactions, thoughts, and past experiences related to the event. Self-validation, like validation from others, can decrease intense stress-related emotions. It can help you identify the problems that contribute to your individual stress levels and to choose coping strategies that are the right fit for you.

Expressing Stress-Related Thoughts and Feelings

Stressors can challenge your basic—and often optimistic—beliefs about yourself and your world. The breakup of a relationship, a serious health problem, making a mistake that has a serious effect on your standing at work, or some other significant change in your life can interfere with your sense of hope that everything will turn out all right. It can also violate your basic assumptions that the world is generally safe and predictable.

Traumatic events and major life changes as well as daily hassles, such as tight work deadlines, criticism, misunderstandings, or doing things that you're not skilled at can create self-doubt that increases your stress symptoms. If you can't integrate a stressful experience into your view of yourself and the world, you will continue to have stress symptoms, such as intrusive thoughts, about the experience.

When you feel that others view your reaction to stressors in your life as invalid, you may hold back your expression of stress-related thoughts and emotions. The pressure to inhibit the expression of your feelings, thoughts, and experiences interferes with your ability to process and adjust to a stressor. Constraining expression of stressful thoughts and feelings can increase intrusive thoughts and prolong mental and physical reactions to stress. In contrast, expressing stressful experiences can improve physical and mental health, decrease stress-related illness, and increase positive emotions (Lepore 1997; Pennebaker, Colder, and Sharp 1990).

Communicating your feelings about stressful circumstances can help you interpret those situations in a meaningful way and better understand confusing aspects of your experience, ultimately reducing the frequency and intensity of stress symptoms (Lepore, Ragan, and Jones 2000).

Attending to your own emotional responses with self-acceptance will help to offset feelings of uncertainty, self-mistrust, or frustration.

Expressing your stress-related emotions helps you construct an account of your experience that makes sense to you. This account can broaden your perspective and help you fit your experience into your view of yourself and the world.

PRACTICE: MULTIPLE-CHOICE EMOTIONAL QUESTIONS

When you are having difficulty articulating an emotional experience, it can help to begin with multiple-choice questions (Linehan 1993a). The following multiple-choice questions are designed to help you begin to articulate your account of the interaction between your internal experience and those circumstances that contribute to your stress levels. Each question might have multiple answers, or no answer may feel like a fit. There are no right or wrong answers to any of the questions.

In a journal or notebook, write out your answers to each of these questions. If all of the answers under a question fit, write them all down. If none fit, then skip the question or write out an answer of your own that's a better fit.

1. What type of situation is triggering your stress response?

    a. *Major life change* (for example, a death or divorce)

    b. *Trauma* (for example, being the victim of abuse or a crime)

    c. *Daily hassles* (for example, physical discomfort, bad weather, or frequent interruptions)

    d. *Uncertainty about the future* (for example, not knowing whether you will get a job or be forgiven by a close friend)

2. How is the situation threatening to you?

    a. I'm physically threatened.

    b. It's a psychological threat; important life goals are threatened.

    c. It's a reminder of negative past experiences.

    d. It contributes to the demands and pressures on me.

3. What thoughts are you having about the situation?

    a. *Self-judgments* (for example, I'm thinking that I am to blame, I'm critical of myself, I'm focused on my inadequacies)

    b. *Judgmental thoughts about others* (for example, I'm thinking that other people are to blame, I'm critical of others, I'm focused on other people's inadequacies)

    c. *Focusing on how things should be or should be different* (for example, I'm thinking that this shouldn't have happened; I feel it should be easier or different for me; I feel that this situation isn't right)

    d. *Dialectical thinking patterns* (for example, I'm able to see multiple viewpoints and accept contradictions; I'm not thinking in extremes and am able to view the situation in its context)

4. Your thoughts tend to be focused on which of these time frames?

    a. *The past* (for example, analyzing what happened or how things might have been different)

    b. *The future* (for example, planning to handle the situation or anticipating negative consequences)

5. What physical aspects of your stress response are you most aware of?

    a. *Acute physical responses* (for example, pounding heart, jumpiness, and dizziness)

    b. *Long-term or chronic physical responses* (for example, fatigue, trouble focusing, and increased susceptibility to colds and illness)

6. What emotions are triggered by the stressful situation?

    a. Fear and anxiety

    b. Anger and frustration

    c. Guilt and shame

    d. Excitement

    e. Sadness and disappointment

    f. A combination of emotions

7. What behavioral urges are you aware of?

    a. Avoiding or running away from the situation

    b. Hiding

    c. Attacking, saying things I might later regret, or hurting others either physically or emotionally

    d. Withdrawing, staying in bed, isolating myself

    e. Connecting with others and finding supportive people

    f. Approaching, solving problems

    g. Using coping skills, strategies to survive a crisis

8. How have I behaved or acted?

    a. Avoided or ran away from the situation

    b. Hid

    c. Attacked, said things I later regretted, or hurt others either physically or emotionally

    d. Withdrew, stayed in bed, and isolated myself

    e. Connected with others and found supportive people

    f. Approached, solved problems

    g. Used coping skills, strategies to survive a crisis

The purpose of this questionnaire is to help you begin to find words to describe your experience. In the next practice exercise, you will use your answers to this questionnaire to help you construct an account of your stressful circumstances. Articulating your emotional reactions in all their complexity helps you make sense of your stressful experiences and incorporate them into your understanding of yourself and the world.

PRACTICE: CONSTRUCT AN ACCOUNT

The expression of stress-related thoughts and feelings has an impact on the symptoms of stress. Constructing an account of your stressful experience not only decreases the intrusive thoughts you have about the experience but also decreases the emotional impact of those thoughts. The purpose of this exercise is not to fix a problem but to simply understand your own experience. If you find yourself beginning to plan for the future while working on this exercise, notice that and bring yourself back to describing your experience.

In the steps that follow, you will create a description of your stressful experience and your internal reaction to that experience. You can do this either by writing the account out in your journal or on a piece of blank paper or by rehearsing your account in your head.

1. Find a quiet time when you won't be interrupted for ten to fifteen minutes. If you are writing your account, get out your journal or paper and a pen or pencil.

2. Begin by describing the experience that is contributing to raising your stress level. It may help to start with your answer to question #1 on the multiple-choice emotion questionnaire and then to expand on that example with specifics that relate to you.

3. Now move on to describing the thoughts you have about this experience. Again, use answers from the questionnaire to get you started. Try to be as specific as possible.

4. Continue describing your reaction to the situation by describing your physical stress response, labeling your emotional reactions, and noting your behavioral urges and actual actions.

5. Review your account and add details as they come to you. Continue to read or review your account over the course of several days or weeks. Over time, you will begin to see patterns, misinterpretations, and meaning. You might identify emotions that you were previously unaware of. A description of both the stressor and your internal experience will help you see how stressors impact your

feelings and thoughts and vice versa—how your feelings and thoughts impact stressful circumstances in your life.

As you make sense of your experience, you will gain trust in your own perspective and be better able to accept your emotional reactions as valid.

You can take this practice one step further by talking to a therapist, loved one, or supportive friend about your experience. The benefits of expressing your thoughts and feelings to others are weakened when they are invalidated, so it's important to choose someone who's a good listener and is able to hear your account without needing to fix your problems or judging your reactions (Lepore, Ragan, and Jones 2000). Emotional support from friends and family, talk therapy, and support groups can all facilitate the process of making sense of stressful experiences.

Understanding Your Own Behaviors

People behave in a wide variety of ways under stress. You may act in ways to effectively manage your stress or may find that you say or do things you later regret or wouldn't have said or done if you had not been under stress. Although you may be critical of your behavior, misplaced and overblown reactions to events often originate in valid responses.

For a stress response to be validated does not mean that the response was an accurate reflection of the events around you or that your reactions to the stressor were okay. For example, maybe you yelled at your children out of frustration because you were late for work and had misplaced your cell phone. You may then have decided that responding to your stress by yelling at your children was not okay but at the same time you understood that given your current work pressures, your stress level and frustration were understandable.

In other words, you can view your stress and your behavior in context and understand it while at the same time holding the belief that you need to change how you react to stress. In fact, the act of viewing your stress in context and understanding your own reactions—extending a kindness and compassion toward yourself—can reduce the intensity of stress-related emotions and change your reactions.

Judgments and Assumptions about Behavior

When under stress, you may have behaved in ways that you wouldn't have when not stressed. It is at these times that we often make judgments and assumptions about our behaviors. Judgments (such as *I should have handled myself better*) and assumptions (such as *Someone else wouldn't have lost it* or *How I handled it was wrong*) don't help you with problem solving and only amplify self-mistrust.

When you have behaved in ways that are not consistent with your values, you may feel anger, guilt, or disappointment in your own behavior. You may tell yourself—and others may tell you—that you "should" behave differently. Questions such as *Why did I do that?* or *How could I have done that?* invalidate the reality of your own experience. The following exercise is based on validation techniques described by Marsha Linehan in her textbook *Cognitive Behavioral Treatment of Borderline Personality Disorder* (Linehan 1993a).

PRACTICE: ACCEPTING YOUR OWN BEHAVIOR

1. Bring to mind a reaction to a stressful experience that you wish had been different. For example, you may have said things that you now regret, lost your temper, or made an impulsive decision. You might choose a situation in which you judge your action harshly. Words such as "should," "wrong," "stupid," "lazy," and "terrible" are indicators of judgmental thinking. Questioning yourself by asking, *What's wrong with me?* or *Why do I behave this way?* are also signals that you wish you'd acted differently.

2. When you think about the way that you behaved, separate understanding how or why you behaved in a particular way from approving of your behavior. Think about the circumstances that contributed to the way you behaved. Try to extend to yourself a kindness and compassion when you view your actions.

3. Try to make sense of your actions given the circumstances, your perceptions, and your stress-related emotions. Can you see your

actions as understandable even while you disapprove of them and believe you need to make changes? Being able to be accepting while understanding a need for and making changes is central to DBT.

4. Acknowledge your displeasure with how you reacted to the situation. It's understandable to feel emotions such as frustration, irritation, embarrassment, and disappointment when you make mistakes and don't act as you wish you would. Allow yourself those feelings and then move on.

Telling yourself that you "shouldn't" act as you have only invalidates your own experience. We all behave differently under stress. The stress response and intense stress-related emotions have an impact on behavior. Holding unrealistic standards for yourself will only perpetuate painful emotions and your stress reaction, and it will interfere with your ability to trust your own responses. Accepting your actions and understanding how they occurred in context, even when you wish you'd acted differently, increases self-understanding and trust.

Self-Validation of Your Thoughts

As with the way you act under stress, you may have thoughts when under stress that you wouldn't have when calm. Common thought processes during times of stress include overwhelming worry; rumination; difficulty controlling your thoughts; reviewing past events, conversations, and actions repetitively; staying stuck in unpleasant thoughts you can't get rid of; negative self-judgment; difficulty making decisions; and intrusive thoughts.

Stressful thinking patterns can exacerbate stressful circumstances. For example, holding unreasonably high expectations or berating yourself for not achieving goals or for focusing too much on negative outcomes can cause you to stay stuck in stress rather than able to move past a stressor.

To be understanding of your stress-related thoughts, it's important to remember that for each event that occurs, we make almost instantaneous judgments about whether it will cause us harm or benefit, whether someone deserves blame or credit, and whether we are able to cope with the stressor. Mistakes in your judgment—say interpreting circumstances as worse than they are or believing that you are unable to cope—have an impact on what emotions you experience and on the intensity and duration of your stress response.

Even if you are angry or frustrated with yourself for thoughts that have kept you trapped in a cycle of stress, you can extend understanding to those very thoughts that are causing you problems.

PRACTICE: EXTENDING SELF-UNDERSTANDING TO YOUR THOUGHTS

It is helpful to explore your interpretations of stressful events, especially if you frequently get stuck reacting to stressors with rigid or distorted thinking that is exaggerated or incompatible with your circumstances. In this exercise you will notice thoughts during times of stress, as you did in chapter 1. Instead of simply noting them, try to extend a sense of self-understanding toward your thinking patterns.

1. Begin by choosing a moment when you feel stressed and bring your attention to your thoughts during that time. Don't try to alter what you're thinking. Just watch your thoughts go by.

2. Tune in to the content of your thoughts and reflect on that content, to yourself, in your mind. For example, you might say to yourself *I'm having worry thoughts about money again* or *There is another intrusive thought about the argument with my sister.* Reflecting on the content of your thoughts might derail your train of thought. That's okay. If that happens, you can complete the exercise the next time you are stressed out.

3. Now extend an understanding to yourself about your own thoughts. Think about your past experiences and your vulnerabilities to stress and the current situation. When you notice thoughts during times of stress, actively think about how even distorted thoughts or excessive worry might make sense. For example, you might think, *My family tended to be critical of mistakes, so it makes sense that I'm stuck in thinking critical thoughts* or *My job is so important to me that it's understandable that I worry when I think it might be threatened.* If

anyone might experience symptoms of stress in your current circumstances, consider telling yourself *It's normal to have psychological symptoms when under stress* or *Anyone might be stuck in unpleasant thoughts after a friend dies unexpectedly*. As you did with your behavior, you can try to make sense of your thoughts—given the circumstances, your perceptions, and your stress-related emotions—and see them as understandable even while you want to change them.

4. Practice, over the course of several days, reflecting on the content of thoughts during times of stress and trying to understand why you have problematic thinking patterns.

Self-understanding won't necessarily change your thinking patterns. However, accepting and acknowledging the content of your thoughts can decrease your reactivity to your stress symptoms.

Wrap-Up

This chapter focused on acknowledging and accepting your emotions, behavior, and thoughts during times of stress. Accepting yourself and your internal reactions to stressors as valid and authentic decreases uncertainty and reduces stress symptoms. Bringing mindful attention to your experience of stress-related emotions, your behavioral reactions to stress, and your thoughts that contribute to stress enables you to better understand the interaction between external stressors and your own internal experience. Understanding and accepting your internal experience as valid can reduce the uncertainty that contributes to ongoing stress and interferes with problem solving and productive action.

CHAPTER 10

Changing Problematic Coping Behaviors

When people are stressed and unhappy, it's usually for good reason. For many, repetitive stressful events and an inability to recover fully from one event before another occurs can lead to impulsive, mood-dependent behavior and inhibit your ability to respond to your problems in an organized and effective way (Linehan 1993a).

When you're stressed, you may not feel you have the time or willpower to cope in healthy ways, such as with exercise, healthy meals, adequate sleep, and pleasant or soothing activities. During these stressful times, unhealthy and destructive coping strategies often provide immediate relief from painful stress-related emotions. Gambling, smoking, eating, shopping, drinking alcohol, and doing nothing are problematic coping strategies people use to manage stress.

A style of problematic coping—say, overeating to soothe frayed nerves, spending money that you don't have, impulsively blowing off a work deadline, ignoring bills or a mortgage payment, or ignoring health issues—can spiral into crisis. Harmful coping strategies don't reduce your stress levels; instead they create additional stress in your life. In fact, over time, a style of problematic coping can become the most significant source of stress in your life: a missed mortgage payment can spiral into foreclosure, drinking alcohol to take the edge off can become an addiction, and so on.

When you realize that you are coping with stress in unhealthy and destructive ways, you may simply tell yourself that you will change. Often, however, changing how you cope with stress is complicated. You may make some common mistakes when faced with recurrent stressors, including believing you are helpless, approaching problems passively, looking to others to solve your problems, trusting others' opinions of the problem as more accurate than your own, oversimplifying the problem and giving up when it isn't immediately solved, trying to solve the problem alone and without help in areas in which you don't have the capability or expertise, or responding impulsively out of emotion rather than effectively from your own priorities.

Just telling yourself to change may not work unless you understand what influences how you act. The strategies in this chapter are designed to help you change problematic coping behaviors. This may mean changing the thoughts and feelings that precede problematic actions, making life-style changes, or learning new skills. These strategies help you clarify your problem behaviors, investigate factors that influence harmful actions, and develop more effective solutions.

In DBT, unhealthy and destructive behaviors are considered problems to be solved. Strategies to solve the problem of these harmful and destructive actions are core to DBT. Harmful behaviors have served a purpose. They have, in some way, helped you cope with overwhelming stress (Linehan 1993a). Now, it's time to get a better understanding of what you are doing and why, so that you can make changes.

Acceptance

Changing problematic patterns of reacting to events and managing your stress levels will require self-acceptance skills. If you find yourself complaining that you shouldn't have to deal with certain problems in your life or harshly judging yourself and your past actions, then you will need to focus on self-acceptance as you try to better understand your behaviors.

Throughout this chapter, you will want to think like an investigative reporter, with your focus on uncovering and acknowledging facts. These might be facts about your current situation, how you act, how you feel, or what you think.

Judging yourself or trying to assign blame will intensify your emotions and make it more likely that you will ignore important facts. Looking at your internal experiences associated with problematic coping can trigger self-criticism that shuts down your analysis. This is an opportunity to practice the mindfulness skills from chapter 6. In particular, you will want to focus on letting go of judgmental thoughts such as *How could I have been so stupid? I'm a failure*, and *I'm a screw-up*. Self-criticism activates shame and embarrassment, which makes it more difficult to understand how your own feelings, thoughts, and behaviors contribute to your current problem.

> As with the strategies in Chapter 8, the strategies in this chapter require a degree of behavioral control. Closely investigating factors associated with destructive and risky behaviors, such as self-injury or suicide attempts, can temporarily increase your experience of painful emotions. It is advisable that you use these strategies only with the help of a professional if you are currently struggling with high-risk behaviors.

Clarify the Problem

Sometimes a problem is obvious: if you are perpetually late to work in the morning, the problem is you're not waking up early enough.

At other times, the problem is not as clear. Take again the example of being perpetually late to work. What if it is part of a larger pattern? What if you're late throughout the day, even when you believe you have adequate time to get where you're going? What if being late causes additional stress for your children or creates tension at work, but, despite making efforts to change, you continue to be late? In this case, the cause of your lateness involves more than at what time you wake up.

• *Leah's Story*

Leah is an office administrator and the mother of three young children. Prior to having children, she maintained a healthy weight with exercise despite eating a lot of sugary foods. Since having kids, Leah has gained sixty-five pounds. Although her food choices previously included too much sugar, she now relies on sugar and caffeine to function during the day. None of the children sleep through the night, so she is perpetually tired. As a result of lay-offs, she has picked up additional responsibilities at work and often finds herself with multiple work demands—all of which must be completed immediately. Exhausted, she eats several donuts throughout the course of a morning, telling herself that she needs the sugar to keep her energy levels up. She regularly eats high-calorie and fatty take-out and fast food. In the evenings she collapses in front of the TV with sugary snacks and desserts, which she tells herself are a reward for getting through another stressful day.

PRACTICE: CLARIFYING YOUR PROBLEM

1. Find a quiet time during the day, take out your journal or a blank piece of paper, and answer the following questions: What makes you think there is a problem? Where is it happening? How is it happening? When is it happening? With whom is it happening?

2. Now create a three- to five-sentence paragraph clearly describing the problem. As you answer questions and gather information, be sure to write it down. Having something written to refer to will assist you later when you return to this information to look for potential solutions.

3. If you've identified several problems, you now need to prioritize and choose the one to begin working on. Put the most important problem at the top. The most important problem is the one that is the most harmful in your life. If a problem puts your life at risk, that is your priority. If you don't have a problem that puts your life at risk, focus on problems that threaten your quality of life—for example, overspending that threatens your ability to pay your mortgage or behaviors at work that threaten your job stability. You will focus on your top-priority problem in the exercises throughout this chapter. After completing the exercises with your top-priority problem, you can return and repeat this process with lower-priority problems.

Leah identified her eating as a top-priority problem. At a recent doctor's visit, she was told that her weight and eating problems put her at high risk for heart disease. Leah's description of her problem looked like this: "I eat sugary and fatty foods throughout the day, and at my current weight am considered obese. I start my day with a sugary breakfast and continue to eat unhealthy foods at home and at work. When my energy is low or I need a break, I eat unhealthy, high-calorie snacks. These foods and my portion sizes exceed the recommended calories for a woman my age. I tend to eat alone, standing at the kitchen counter while the kids watch TV, at my desk at work, or in the car."

Remember that you've been doing the best you can up until this point. Notice feelings that interfere with your motivation to solve this problem and let them pass. Gathering information is crucial to changing how you cope with stress.

Investigating Factors That Influence Harmful Actions

You must explore your internal experience, including your feelings, the physical reactions in your body, and your thoughts, to better understand the interaction between external stressors and your harmful actions. This self-analysis can be one of the most difficult and complicated aspects of changing problem behaviors. It involves looking at your internal thoughts and feelings as well as examining your individual vulnerabilities and the specific situations that set off a problematic series of actions.

Uncovering What Precedes Harmful Actions

Problems don't just come out of nowhere. Something happens that triggers a stress response. The interaction between that stressful situation and your internal experience of stress leads up to your harmful actions. With DBT, you will want to gather information about the stress-related feelings, thoughts, and physical reactions that come before a harmful action. Like the stress log you created in chapter 1, the next two exercises require you to explore events that trigger a stress response and to look closely at the feelings, thoughts, and behaviors you have in response to that event. These exercises will take that exploration a step further by asking you to examine an initial event leading up to harmful or destructive actions and the entire series of thoughts and feelings set off by that event.

PRACTICE: WHEN DID THE PROBLEM BEGIN?

To make changes, you must pinpoint the external stressful situation that set off a succession of events and internal experiences that ultimately resulted in an unhealthy or destructive act. Identifying the beginning of problematic actions gives focus to the rest of your self-investigation.

1. Find a quiet time during the day and take out your journal or a blank piece of paper. Read through your description of your problem actions. Choose one specific time when the problem occurred. For example, Leah chose to focus on one specific morning when she overate while at her desk at work.

2. Think about and write down what happened that set you down the path that ended with problematic actions. It may help to think about and write down answers to the following questions: "What set the problem off?" "What stressors was I dealing with when the problem started?" "What was I doing that set me on a path of problematic coping?" "Why did the problem happen at that specific time, instead of at another time or on another day?"

3. If you're having trouble figuring out what set off the problem, take a guess as to roughly what situation might have set off the harmful action. The goal is to figure out what external stressor set off the series of internal experiences that led up to problematic actions. You may have to examine several instances of the problem behavior before you can clearly identify the stressful situation that sets it off.

A stressful event happens. The interaction of that initial stressful event with your individual internal experience and any subsequent circumstances is the focus of your investigation. A better appreciation of what stressors precede harmful coping behaviors will help you understand your own behavior and will provide a focus for making changes.

PRACTICE: INTERNAL EXPERIENCES THAT PRECEDE HARMFUL ACTIONS

This exercise continues to explore the sequence of events and experiences that precede unhealthy or destructive actions. These are your individual experiences that take place between the stressful event that sets things off and your harmful action.

1. Focus on the same specific occurrence of a harmful action that you identified in the previous exercise. Using your journal or a blank piece of paper, write down any feelings that you remember having after a stressor occurred that set you on a path to problematic coping. As you think about how you felt during and after the stressful situation, write about any emotions that you can remember from the time of the stressor until immediately before you acted in an unhealthy or destructive way.

2. Write out physical sensations for the same time period. Think about how your body felt. For example, were you feeling tense, keyed up, or drained of energy? Try to put a name to the emotion associated with the feelings in your body. If you can't identify an emotion, take a wild guess. Think about other physical feelings you might have had in your body, such as hunger pains, a headache, or dizziness.

   Leah's examination of her feelings looked like this: "Immediately before eating, my body felt completely drained and physically tired. I was sluggish, my arms were heavy. I felt like I couldn't concentrate. I'm not entirely sure of the emotions, but I'd guess anxious, overwhelmed, and abandoned."

3. Now take a look at your thoughts associated with the problem actions. You'll want to look at the thoughts that occur just before you usually act in problematic ways. Ask yourself what you are telling yourself that contributes to the feelings you identified above. What goes through your mind right before you act? Think about whether you're aware of your thoughts at the time.

   Thoughts that contributed to overeating and reaching for unhealthy foods for Leah included *I need this, I'm tired and need the*

energy, These are unreasonable expectations, and there's no way I can do this,
I've got too much to do and I deserve something special, I've got no help, and I
can't handle it.

4. Now turn your attention to how you act, when you are feeling and
   thinking in the ways you've already described. What do you feel
   like doing? What do you actually do?

   Leah felt like giving up. Instead she ate.

5. Put it all in order. Although it's hard to create a linear series of
   experiences that lead from a stressor to an action, try the best you
   can. Knowing how your feelings and thoughts interact with events
   that end in problematic behaviors will help you understand your
   actions and find ways to change. To put the sequence of your
   experiences in order, make two columns in your journal or on a
   piece of paper. In the first column write "Stressful situation."
   Below that write "Feeling in body," and then "Thoughts,"
   "Emotion," "Behavioral urge," and "Action." Repeat these categories two or three times (or as many times as necessary) until the
   final action is the harmful act you're focused on investigating.

   Leah's list began like this.

Stressful situation	*While I was working on several projects that I was already worried I wouldn't have time to finish, my boss asked me to immediately reschedule a meeting that had been very difficult to set up. Rescheduling the meeting would take time, make me late on the other projects, and mean that I would have to deal with several different people who would be annoyed and had been demeaning to me in the past.*
Feeling in body	*I felt sluggish, exhausted.*
Thoughts	*He has no idea how much work this is. I'll never get it done.*
Emotion	*Unappreciated*

Behavioral urge	*Cry*
Action	*Picked up phone to make calls, left message.*
Stressful situation	*Got first irate phone call back.*
Feeling in body	*Tension in my face*
Thoughts	*I don't deserve this.*
Emotion	*Anger*
Behavioral urge	*Tell my boss to do it himself*
Action	*Made and took more calls. Listened to more frustrated people.*
Stressful situation	*Got a call chewing me out for not having the projects done that I'd been working on.*
Feeling in body	*Muscle tension, knotted stomach*
Thoughts	*I need a break.* *This isn't fair.*
Emotion	*Anxiety*
Behavioral urge	*Escape*
Harmful action	*Went to the break room and ate three donuts, got a coffee with heavy cream, and took a bagel with cream cheese back to my desk to eat while I worked.*

You can see several things from Leah's initial list. External stressors continued to occur and had an impact on her internal experience. In addition, her list contains quite a bit of information about her internal experience, and if she spent more time on it, she could likely come up with more and more information. Internal reactions to stressors happen quickly. That and continued external stressors can mean that you have a lot of information that can go on your list. Do your best to flesh it out and get the important facts—about what happened and your internal reaction to what happened. The information you gather here will help you identify patterns in how you react.

Identifying Patterns

When you want to change how you act, it helps to find patterns in the succession of experiences that occur between a stressor and a harmful action. It's usually our patterns of reacting that make us more likely to repeat a problem behavior over and over. If you're able to alter one of these patterns, you may no longer have the urge to do things such as drink too much alcohol to take the edge off or spend too much money.

To find patterns, you will need to repeat the exercises above several times. Each time you act in a harmful way, to yourself or others, you can repeat your analysis, identifying what set off problem actions and the connections between your feelings, thoughts, and external events. It is when you write out your internal experience over and over that you will see patterns. For example, you might find that you always feel lonely before binge eating, that you make the assumption you can't control your spending before you overspend, or that you refuse help from coworkers before you have angry conflicts with your partner.

PRACTICE: PATTERNS IN FACTORS THAT INFLUENCE HARMFUL COPING

1. Take out the exercises in which you identified your internal experiences that lead up to the problem as well as when your problematic behavior began. Read them over, looking for patterns.

2. Look for *automatic responses*. Examples of automatic responses are always getting stressed in unfamiliar circumstances, getting overly emotional and impulsive in each instance the behavior occurs, continually avoiding conflict, ignoring or glossing over the problem, refusing help, and running away from the problem.

3. Look for *gaps in your ability*. For example, you may go along with others and find yourself drinking too much alcohol because you don't know how to socialize without drinking; you may not know how to eat healthy portions that fill you up, which can contribute to overeating; or you may be unaware of programs designed to help you save money, which can help you curb your overspending.

4. Look for *problematic beliefs and fears*. Examples of such beliefs and fears include believing that you can't stand being criticized or rejected by others, expecting that you will not get the help you need, and assuming that you are helpless and have no control.

5. Look for *vulnerability factors*. These are factors that may not have directly contributed to the problem but that made it more likely to occur. Vulnerability factors include lifestyle choices as well as current emotions and stressors not directly related to the problem. Examples of vulnerability factors include getting too little sleep, not eating a balanced diet, and having recently experienced a trauma or other stressful major life event.

6. Try to identify at least two to three of these patterns. Again, if you're not sure, take a guess. It's not necessary to be certain, right now. The goal is to be open to looking for and considering potential patterns. Eventually this openness will allow you to find those patterns that influence your harmful actions.

Finding patterns in your reactions to the stressors that precede harmful behaviors will give you a clear focus for developing effective solutions. If you're able to change a pattern of reacting, you can alter the sequence of events that leads up to your harmful actions.

Developing Effective Solutions

Now that you've gathered a lot of information, it's time to switch gears and begin to look at how to change your actions. You will want to approach this part of the process with a spirit of openness and opportunity. At this point in problem solving, you need to explore options at every turn. Don't discard any possibility.

Although you want to be open to all possibilities for change, you want your solutions to be self-focused. By this I mean that you want to focus on changes that *you* make rather than on changes in the environment. For example, Leah wants to gain more control over her work demands. Rather than focusing on solving her problem by changing her boss, which is not necessarily a solution she has the power to influence, she needs to keep her focus on specific environmental and behavioral changes that she can influence. For example, Leah can focus on communicating to her boss about her work demands and how she manages her schedule. She can open up a conversation with him about how best to meet her other work demands and still get his needs met. Leah can't make her boss change, but she can change how she communicates, which may mean that she gets her needs met. If that doesn't work, she will have to look for other solutions that she can affect.

PRACTICE: BRAINSTORMING CHANGES IN STRESS REACTIONS

1. Take out your previous exercises from this chapter and begin by asking yourself, *What would I have to change to make my life better?* or *What would have to change for the situation to improve?* Make a list of your answers. Try to focus on changes to your thoughts and feelings as well as to external events.

2. Consider each piece of information that you identified in earlier exercises as a potential opportunity to do something differently. For example, Leah identified the thought *I don't deserve this* and her feeling of anger as opportunities to respond differently. She could use strategies from chapter 2 to change her thinking as well as mindfulness strategies from chapter 6 to notice her feelings without reacting to them.

3. Pick five points for change in the sequence of events and internal experiences that precedes a problem behavior and try to generate two to three solutions for each point. For example, you might choose to find solutions to the lack of sleep and health problems that make you vulnerable to acting impulsively. You may also choose to focus on changing thoughts that contribute to anxious feelings and reducing how often you experience the stressful event that sets off the problem.

4. Don't limit your list of solutions. With DBT, you tell yourself that "quantity breeds quality" (Linehan 1993a). You can narrow your list and choose the best solution for you later. Right now, focus on

creating as many options as possible. Look around you and see what others have done to solve similar problems. Go through earlier chapters in this book and look for possible strategies you might use to help you respond differently. Resist the urge to reject ideas or to tell yourself that you couldn't do what someone else has done.

5. As you review patterns in your reactions to stressful events, identify strategies from earlier chapters in this book that might be alternative ways of responding.

6. Ask trusted friends and family for ideas.

Leah's five points for change in the sequence of events that preceded overeating were as follows:

- An automatic response of avoiding conflict by not communicating her needs

- Having unhealthy foods readily available

- The vulnerability factor of getting too little sleep

- The gap in her ability to create healthy meals because she didn't understand her nutritional needs

- Her continual self-criticism and judgmental thinking

For each of those five problem points, she created a list of potential changes she could make. For example, she listed times that she didn't assert herself, how she could bring up her needs with other people, and healthier foods she could have readily available. She researched healthier options at fast-food restaurants she frequently went to and listed steps she could take to get information about healthier eating habits. She knew that being perpetually tired made her vulnerable to unhealthy eating but wasn't sure how to make changes in that. She wrote out where she could get ideas on how to get more sleep—for instance, from other working mothers who had struggled with children waking at night. Finally, she identified exercises, particularly those in chapter 6 (Cultivating Mindfulness) and in chapter 2 (Unwinding Your Mind), to deal with her self-criticism and judgmental thinking.

At this point, you want to generate as many solutions as possible. In the end, you will have as many as fifteen different potential changes that you can make. You may make only a few of these changes or you may make many of them, but having come up with multiple options allows you to choose the course of action that is the best fit for you.

Evaluate Strategies for Coping Effectively

There are many potential strategies for changing your patterns of reacting to stressful circumstances. Sometimes, given time alone, we change how we act. But usually we have to take a more active role in solving problematic reactions to stressors if we want to change harmful and destructive behaviors. Simply ignoring the problem reactions or waiting for things to change typically makes the situation worse.

The challenge is to determine which strategies will work the best for you. You want to choose strategies that fit your strengths and skills, as well as those that have the best potential to be effective. Although you are looking to make changes that fit your strengths and skills, changing harmful and destructive behaviors is likely to require you to try things that are out of your comfort zone. If coping with stress in healthy ways was easy, you would already be doing it.

PRACTICE: EVALUATING STRATEGIES FOR CHANGE

1. Take out the list of potential changes in your reactions to stress that you generated in the previous exercise and review the changes and strategies.

2. With each potential change or new strategy you might try, ask yourself what you expect to happen. Consider both your short-term and long-term expectations with each possible solution. For example, one potential solution Leah identified was asserting her needs and negotiating with others to better balance the demands made on her. Her expectations were that some people would respond to her requests, and that she would be motivated to assert

herself with these people. At the same time, she expected that others would not make asserting herself easy and that she would struggle to express herself with these people.

In the short term, she expected that sticking up for herself would create additional stress and tension because the people around her were used to her picking up the slack and getting things done. However, in the long term, she expected that reducing the demands on her time and energy would decrease her stress levels and decrease the feelings of being unappreciated and abandoned that consistently preceded overeating.

3. Now ask yourself how realistic your expectations are. Try to step back from your emotional attachment to your expectations and activate wise mind. When you are centered and not feeling defensive, ask yourself whether you tend to be overly optimistic or tend to expect the worst. Review your expectations to determine whether you feel they are skewed either positively or negatively. It may help to ask a trusted person in your life for help.

4. As you evaluate different strategies, make a note of negative expectations or problems. You don't want to get stuck in negative expectations, but at the same time, you don't want to ignore them. Instead ask yourself how you might overcome the obstacles you could face when you implement a change.

If one or two strategies aren't becoming clear possibilities, you may get frustrated and feel like giving up. Allow yourself a little frustration and then return to the process. Stubborn problems take time. Keep in mind that you may need to learn some new skills or get help to make changes in your reactions to stress.

Choose to Change

At some point in the process, you'll need to choose to make changes. If you are lucky, your analysis will make the strategies you'll use clear. However, it's more likely that you will need to choose several potential strategies.

It may seem that there are no good alternatives. If this is the case, you have two options. You can return to clarifying and evaluating your harmful or destructive behavior with the goal of generating more possible strategies. Or, if you feel you've done a thorough evaluation, you can choose the strategies that you consider the least bad.

Sometimes making a change will require you to suffer some pain and difficulty. Leah had a very strong desire to please people and had always had trouble asserting her needs, disappointing people, or causing frustration for others. She knew that asserting herself was going to take an act of will and would require her to tolerate the pain of causing other people discomfort. This was one of the hardest changes for Leah to make in the areas she had listed, but she also believed it was the one that would have the most impact in the long term. Like Leah, you may need to give up some things you hold dear and try new behaviors that are uncomfortable in order to change your harmful behavior.

ANTICIPATE ROADBLOCKS

Once you've begun, you don't want to get thrown offtrack. To keep focused, you must anticipate potential obstacles. Encountering a problem can trigger strong emotions like fear, anxiety, and anger. When you begin down a difficult path and find an obstruction, it's normal to feel annoyed and exasperated. You can also expect to worry that this, too, will not lead to healthier coping.

Although it's impossible to anticipate all potential impediments, you can plan for some. Knowing that problems may arise will keep you flexible and ready to adjust when necessary. You want to keep focused on doing what works rather than get sidetracked by emotions and negative thinking.

GET SPECIFIC, GET PRACTICE, AND GET STARTED

To make changes, you need to have a specific plan. For Leah to just decide to eat better is an oversimplification that invalidates the complexity of the factors that contribute to her overeating. She has to get specific about how she will eat better. You're much more likely to actually make and follow through on changes if you've planned how you'll do it.

PRACTICE: PLANNING TO MAKE CHANGES

1. Write down the top two or three changes you want to make. Choose those changes that you think are the best fit for you and to which you feel you can commit. Make sure you believe that these changes will actually have an impact on the harmful actions you're trying to alter. Leah knew that having healthy foods in the house would make her feel as if she was working on her overeating, but she didn't think that healthy foods alone would change her eating habits. She chose to have healthy foods available as one solution but knew she had to pair it with other solutions in order for it to be effective. If no strategies seem good, choose those that are the least bad.

2. Look at the changes you've identified and write down any potential roadblocks that come to mind. How can you adjust when you run up against a problem? What might you do to steer around problems that could come up? You don't need to anticipate every obstacle, but having a few alternate strategies in mind will help you remain flexible and will keep you from giving up when faced with a setback.

3. Write down specific action steps. Where will you begin? When? What specifically do you need to do? How will you manage your anxiety along the way?

4. Break the steps down and plan out what you need to do each day and week. Go over precisely what you need to do. Leah identified when she would go shopping, what she would buy, and when she would prepare healthy foods that she could have readily available. She also rehearsed talking to her boss before she approached him about managing her workload. She then chose a time to have the discussion when they wouldn't be interrupted so she would have the time to fully articulate her needs and discuss options.

Change may feel overwhelming at first. But when you break changes down into small, manageable steps, you may find that each task is difficult but not impossible.

The Impact of Emotion

If you've gone through the exercises in this chapter and found that you're unable to identify changes that you could make, the issue may not be that change is impossible. Negative emotions like fear, sadness, anger, and shame may be interfering with your ability to see clearly, make decisions, and attempt different resolutions (Linehan 1993a).

When you're feeling good, you tend to have more ideas and can be more flexible in how you approach changes. Flexible thinking is partly about being able to actively choose strategies that fit your goals and that are adaptive, creative, and relevant. Flexibility allows you to move beyond automatic and habitual ways of seeing the world and open up to new ways of thinking. It allows you to let go of rigid rules and unnecessary restrictions you place on yourself and enables you to come up with effective solutions. When you're feeling good, you're better able to see the world as it is, not as you think it should be.

On the other hand, when your stress levels are high and you're experiencing stress-related emotions such as sadness, anger, or anxiety, you're more likely to see limited possibilities. When you're experiencing strong emotions, you can expect problem solving to go more slowly and be more difficult.

The exercises in chapter 3 that are designed to get your body into a more accepting state can also help you manage your stress-related emotions. A calmer state of mind allows you to clarify the situation and see new solutions.

Building Resilience

If you've habitually avoided problems or been unsuccessful in your early attempts to make changes, you may feel that there simply are no strategies that will help. Bad outcomes early on can result in a lack of confidence in your ability to find solutions at all (Linehan 1993a).

People who have experienced good outcomes tend to see themselves as effective and capable. With each good outcome, their confidence in themselves builds. If they experience a failure, their confidence in their abilities motivates them to continue to try until they succeed. Very often after several attempts to make changes, they do succeed.

On the other hand, if you've struggled early on, your doubt in yourself can make it more likely that you will give up if your first efforts to make changes aren't successful. People who view themselves as competent and capable also often experience initial failure. The difference is that they maintain a commitment to solving their problem, even in the face of obstacles. However, if you interpret your first setback to mean that you will never successfully make changes, you are likely to give up before trying again.

There is no one "right" way to respond to life's difficulties. Whatever way you choose, the ability to be flexible in your responses to stressful circumstances and to endure despite difficulties is key to achieving life goals. *Resilience*—the willingness to get up once you have fallen and try again—can be learned. It is often the difference between success and defeat.

Wrap-Up

When you're stressed, you may not feel you have the time or willpower to cope in healthy ways. During stressful times, unhealthy and destructive coping strategies often provide immediate relief from painful stress-related emotions. But using harmful coping strategies to distract yourself from stress can create more problems and escalate into crisis. This chapter focused on changing problematic coping behaviors (such as overeating or spending too much money), helping you explore factors that lead up to problem behaviors, and identifying alternative responses to life circumstances that can impact your behavior.

In DBT, harmful actions are investigated to better understand them and to make your choices about how you react to stressful circumstances more effective. The strategies in this chapter are intended to help you clarify harmful actions, investigate the relationship between external stressors and your internal experiences, and develop healthy ways of coping with stressors.

Change can be difficult and at times disheartening. Approaching problems with a willingness to overcome obstacles and setbacks can be the key to accomplishing your goals. In chapter 11, you'll explore strategies for staying hopeful and motivated during the process of change.

CHAPTER 11

Staying Motivated, Hopeful, and On Track

Much of this book is focused on making changes. You may have practiced making changes in many different aspects of your life, including how you think about stressful life events, how you eat, how much you exercise, your daily routines, your interactions with others, how you soothe yourself during a crisis, or the focus of your attention. All of these changes can help you cope with your stress in healthy ways, reduce the overall intensity and duration of your acute stress response, and reduce the amount of chronic stress in your life.

But making and maintaining change is hard. The purpose of this last chapter is to teach you strategies to maintain motivation, hope, and consistency as you practice new strategies.

To stay motivated during times of change, you need to learn to manage your environment rather than submit passively to it. Making and maintaining a less stressful life requires that your environment promote positive change. This chapter helps to clarify the factors in your environment that have an impact on your motivation to change.

It also contains strategies for understanding the forces that control your behavior, setting goals, tracking your progress, and creating rewards for your accomplishments. It teaches you how to observe your own limits, which decreases the likelihood that you'll become "burned out" by excessive demands.

The process of learning to change behavior is a much-studied topic in psychology. There are textbooks and psychology courses devoted to understanding the external forces that influence our behavior (see, for example, Lieberman 1990). In DBT, understanding and managing the external factors that influence behaviors is considered essential to making and maintaining positive changes (Linehan 1993a).

Understanding the Forces That Influence Your Behavior

When you're trying to change how you manage your stress, it's important to understand the forces that influence how you act. What happens immediately after you behave in a particular way, your motivation, and your insight into these forces all have an impact on whether you will make and sustain changes that improve your ability to cope with your stress levels.

Positive Reinforcement

Often when we're trying to change behavior, we ignore the contingencies already operating in our lives. *Contingencies*—two events that tend to occur together—can have a great impact on how you act and how difficult it is to make changes. For example, a child's misbehavior might get a teacher's attention. So misbehavior and attention from the teacher are contingencies that are linked for the child. In other examples, asserting yourself might provoke a supervisor's criticism, or each time you practice mindfulness, your partner might make a supportive comment. These pairings—misbehavior and attention, assertiveness and criticism, and mindfulness practice and support—influence whether you will repeat an action. In each case, what happened along with or immediately after an action has an impact on whether you will continue to behave in that particular way.

Positive reinforcement is a powerful way to change behavior. Even a behavior that occurs irregularly can be increased with positive reinforcement. A *reinforcer* is a contingency that makes it more likely that you will repeat an action, so positive reinforcement is something you want. Getting a bonus for completing a project at work is positive reinforcement. Praise, food (for better or worse), a hug, validation, a bubble bath, or a smile can all be positive reinforcers.

Negative reinforcers also have an impact on behavior. In negative reinforcement, you behave in a particular way to avoid something you don't like. For example, you may get to work on time and complete a project to avoid a supervisor's disapproval. A honking horn, criticism, and intense negative emotions can all be negative reinforcers.

Both positive and negative reinforcers are already operating in all of our lives, but most of us are unaware of how they influence our motivation to make and stick to changes. The ways people in our lives respond to us, for example, are extremely powerful reinforcers. Criticism, disapproval, and the disgust of others are powerful negative reinforcers that we'll work hard to avoid, while attention, praise, validation, care, concern, and support from others tend to be positive reinforcers that can boost certain behaviors.

Not only are we often unaware of these reinforcers, we also rarely make a conscious effort to arrange for them to support the positive changes we want to make. Too frequently we rely on chance and self-punishment (in the form of self-criticism) to motivate changes.

Attending to the contingencies operating in your life and switching from self-criticism for not achieving your goals to positive reinforcement can be all that it takes to help you make and maintain the changes you want. Rather than criticizing yourself for not making changes, or for not changing quickly enough, you focus instead on arranging positive reinforcers—say, self-encouragement, treating yourself to a break from an undesirable task, a talk with a supportive friend, or a few quiet moments alone—to co-occur with or follow any change.

PRACTICE: REWARDING YOURSELF FOR POSITIVE CHANGE

Positive reinforcement can come in many forms, but it's important that it be something you see as positive and that it occur relatively close in time to the behavior that you're trying to encourage. To increase the positive reinforcement that is paired with making changes, it helps to identify reinforcement over which you have some influence.

1. In your journal or on a blank piece of paper, write down potential positive reinforcers. Your own internal self-talk and the responses of people around you, often in the form of attention or praise, are powerful reinforcers. Other reinforcers include items and activities, like a favorite food, a special perfume, a walk outside, or time to focus on a hobby.

2. Now focus on some of the changes you want to make to improve your stress levels. How will you pair the reinforcer with the desired change such as asserting yourself, increasing mindfulness practice, or eating a balanced diet? What do you need to do to make sure this reinforcement is available and occurs close in time to the behavior?

There are often long-term positives, such as reduced stress levels, improved energy and mood, and improved relationships, that are associated with making changes. However, focusing on reinforcement in the short term is important. In the shorter term, contingencies can make changes difficult. For example, it's much easier and more comfortable to sit in front of the TV than to practice mindfulness exercises. It's hard to get motivated by the longer-term positive effects of regular mindfulness practice when, in the short term, you are comfortable and interested in the program you are watching on TV.

Motivation

Whether you behave in any one particular way—say, whether you get up in the morning and exercise—depends on your motivation to obtain a certain result. Which particular result doesn't matter so long as you perceive it to be positive; for example, you may be motivated to exercise by a desire for increased muscle, weight loss, stress reduction, or a feeling of well-being.

The degree of your motivation depends on the attractiveness and immediacy of the result. You will work harder for a more attractive result. And although we're capable of delaying gratification, a more immediate result is more motivating. Take again the example of exercise. If your stress levels are very high and exercising significantly reduces your stress, you will be motivated to exercise to achieve stress reduction. Often, in the case of exercise, improvements in how you feel occur after you're done exercising, while changes in weight and your body can take weeks or months to achieve. Because results are not immediate, motivating yourself to get started and to exercise consistently is difficult, despite its long-term positive effects.

Awareness and Insight

The first step in changing your motivation is awareness. For example, if you frequently lose your temper, are you aware of the contingencies that may be bolstering an angry response? Sure, you might feel guilty later or regret an outburst, but what happens in the immediate aftermath? Remember that contingencies are paired with or immediately follow a behavior. In the example of losing your temper, do people back off in that moment? Are you left alone, or do people bend to your will in that instant? Any behavior that occurs frequently, whether it's one you're happy with or one you want to change, likely occurs with something else that strengthens your behavior. Awareness of and insight into the forces that are making you more likely to behave in one way over another allow you to make changes in yourself and your environment to support the actions and behavior that you want. Even when you can't change all the factors that influence your behavior—you can't necessarily change how others respond to you, for example—insight into the short-term consequences that are supporting an undesirable action can help keep you motivated for the positive but longer-term outcomes.

There are numerous ways to change your motivation to respond differently. Take the example in which people bend to your will when you lose your temper. You are better able to make changes once you become aware that people giving way to you is part of what sustains your problem with your temper. Some examples of how you might then make changes follow:

- *To motivate yourself to remain calm during times of disagreement,* call to mind longer-term positives of calm interactions, such as greater intimacy or improved relationships. (You might want to write these longer-term positives down or have rehearsed them in your mind before approaching a potential conflict.)

- *To increase calm reactions toward others,* you can create short-term positive reinforcement for yourself every time you discuss differences without losing your temper.

- *To reduce the likelihood of people giving way to you,* you can change how you approach differences; for example, you might write out your concerns while you are calm and send them in an e-mail before approaching someone for a conversation.

- *To decrease the possibility that you will lose your temper,* you can change the context in which you approach differences—for example, choose to have conversations in situations in which you rarely yell (say while in a restaurant, library, or while taking a walk).

- *To lessen the influence of people giving way to you,* you can change your goals. Instead of trying to get your way, approach differences with the sole goal of gaining a better understanding of the other person's point of view.

This awareness, along with consciously making changes to strengthen and support the positive behavior change you want, will make it much more likely that you will stick to healthy coping strategies.

PRACTICE: NOTICING CONTINGENCIES

1. Choose a behavior that you want to change in order to reduce your stress levels. For example, you might want to increase your use of a particular stress-reduction strategy in this book—say, going to sleep earlier, getting more exercise, increasing your mindfulness practice, or increasing the frequency of pleasant events in your life.

2. Over the course of the next week, pay attention to the times when you intend to change the behavior but don't as well as to the times when you do make the change.

3. Make a note of the contingencies that occurred when you intended to change the behavior but did not. For example, when you told a friend that you were going to take some time to practice mindfulness, did he make a dismissive comment? Or when you intended to go to bed earlier, did a funny program come on the TV? At the end of each day, it may help to take out your journal or a piece of paper and write down what you noticed.

4. Make a note of the contingencies that occurred when you did engage in the behavior. Notice both the positive and negative reinforcers that occurred with or immediately after any change that you made. Again, it may help to write down what you noticed at the end of each day.

5. At the end of the week, review what you have noticed about the contingencies currently operating in your life around this change you want to make. What impact do you think those contingencies have on your motivation? Which ones make it less likely that you will make a change, and which ones make it more likely?

Becoming aware of those times when you get something positive that you want and when something occurs that you want to avoid will help you see why it can be so hard to make some changes. With awareness, you can begin to structure your life to support positive change.

Setting and Achieving Goals

To begin to make changes in your life, you must first identify goals. To have staying power, a goal generally needs to solve a problem. Your goals might include any of the strategies in this book; for example, you might want to change how you respond during stressful circumstances or how you think about a stressful life event. You may want to focus on a particular strategy such as to improve your ability to let go of painful emotions, to increase positive life experiences, or to change problematic behavior patterns. Once you choose a goal, you can break it down into manageable steps.

Shaping—Taking Steps toward Change

It can be overwhelming when you want to make changes in your life. It is especially difficult when there are several areas in which you want to make changes or the change is substantial. *Shaping* is the process of making changes in manageable, incremental steps. The process involves establishing small, intermediate goals that bring you closer and closer to your ultimate goal.

BEGINNING TO NOTICE BEHAVIOR THAT IS ALREADY PRESENT

Shaping begins with identifying and reinforcing times when behavior that is consistent with your goal is already present. For example, if you feel constantly worried and overwhelmed by intense stress and multiple demands, you might set a goal to increase mindfulness in your everyday life. Even if you don't yet practice intentional mindfulness exercises, there are times when you do act mindfully—say, by letting go of judgmental thoughts or by fully participating in an activity. In this example, you would begin the shaping process by noticing those times of mindfulness—even if they are very brief—and reinforcing them. You can reinforce them with anything that is likely to increase their occurrence, which might include thinking encouraging thoughts, self-praise, or some other sort of reward.

SEEING CHANGE AS A CONTINUUM

As you continue the process of shaping change, notice and reward yourself for gradual steps toward your goals. Expecting total or immediate change sets you up to overlook those small steps that build toward considerable life changes. To maintain motivation and progress, it is most effective to notice small movements toward a goal.

The process of making changes in DBT is not seen as either black or white, success or failure. Instead, change is viewed on a continuum. At one end of the continuum is "No change at all" and at the other is "Reaching your goal." In the middle are those small, intermediate steps that lead to your goal. These small changes build upon each other, providing reinforcement at each step you've accomplished. Once you feel confident with one change, you move on to the next incremental change in the continuum. If your motivation weakens or you lose focus, you return to earlier steps in the continuum.

Change is often more about persistence than about having an "aha" moment. Positive reinforcement is crucial to maintaining the motivation to keep making the changes you want in your life.

PRACTICE: MAKING A CHANGE

1. Take out your journal or a blank piece of paper and ask yourself the question, *What would have to change to improve my stress levels?* or *What strategies do I want to try to reduce my stress levels?* If you have a particular problem that is creating stress in your life, you may ask, *What would have to change to solve this problem or for the situation to improve?* Write down your answers to these questions.

2. Ask yourself what contingencies help maintain your current actions. Are there any contingencies that reinforce change? How can you influence the contingencies around this change to support the actions you want? For example, can you talk about your goal with people who tend to be more supportive rather than with those who are pessimistic about your ability to make changes? Can you pair getting into bed a half-hour earlier with a few minutes of reading a good book?

3. Identify and reinforce times when you are already engaging in the desired behavior. For example, if your goal is to increase mindfulness in your life, notice when you are fully present in an activity or when you get refocused after a distraction. Even talking about or thinking about practicing mindfulness is a step toward becoming more mindful. How can you positively reinforce (for yourself) what you are already doing? It may help to look at the reinforcers you identified in the exercise Practice: Rewarding Yourself for Positive Change and identify how you can pair those positive reinforcers with the changes you want to make.

4. Write out a continuum of change. At the top of a blank piece of paper or a page in your journal, write out what it would look like to not make any changes at all. At the bottom of the page, write out what it would look like to achieve your goal. Now fill the space in between with small changes and flexible minigoals all in support of your larger goal.

   For the mindfulness example above, you might start with the goal to increase your mindfulness of your stress levels. At the top of the page you might write, "Being distracted, multitasking, running on automatic pilot, and experiencing stress without being aware of it until it is intense." At the bottom of the page, you might write, "Being focused, doing one thing at a time, being aware of my stress levels as they occur."

On the continuum between the two, you might include something like this:

- "Notice when I'm already mindful during the day."

- "Practice an intentional mindfulness once a week."

- "Practice breathing exercises."

- "Notice stress-related changes in my body, such as when my muscles tense."

- "Practice breathing exercises when I'm overwhelmed by emotion."

- "Practice putting my stressful experiences into words."

Continue in this way until the small steps result in the larger goal of increasing mindfulness of emotion.

5. Begin to implement the changes you've identified. Start with noticing and reinforcing behaviors that are already present and then move on to the smallest step on your continuum. Remember that changes take time, persistence, and reinforcement. Moving both forward and backward on your continuum is to be expected.

Actively managing the contingencies that influence your behavior can help you stay motivated to make changes. An awareness of and focus on the small steps that collectively lead to substantial change can help you maintain hope. What happens immediately after both healthy and unhealthy attempts to cope has a significant impact on whether you will repeat a behavior and how often you will repeat it. You have an ability to influence those factors.

Observing Your Limits

Keeping your sanity in the midst of competing demands requires the ability to observe your own limits and those of others. With DBT, it is assumed that, whether legitimately or otherwise, people often want or need something from you that you are unable or unwilling to give (Linehan 1993a). According to DBT, the ability to limit excessive demands on others as well as the ability to know and observe your own limits is necessary in any relationship.

Continually stretched limits cause extreme stress. Extreme stress leads to reactivity and interferes with your ability to clearly think through how to resolve a problem. You can view stretched limits as a problem in the fit between what someone needs from you and what you're willing or able to provide. There is no "correct" balance between what you need and what others need from you. Seeing your stretched limits as a problem to solve can reduce your anxiety and help you get more active in finding a solution.

Here are some components of observing your limits:

- *Self-awareness.* Everyone has personal limits. Reflect on what you are willing to do and what expectations are tolerable for you in situations that push your limits. Remember that limits change over time. For example, unfinished work, misunderstandings, illness, and discomfort can impact your personal limits on any given day. What might have been tolerable before may not be anymore.

- *Telling people your limits ahead of time.* You can avoid a lot of problems by letting people know your limits ahead of time. Giving a supervisor ample notice that you'll need two weeks off in December for your sister's wedding or that you need to leave early on Tuesdays to get your daughter from school make collaboration more likely. Letting your partner know well in advance that you've got extra work allows him or her to mentally prepare and help you manage the increased responsibilities during that time.

- *Stretching your limits temporarily.* Sometimes work, social, or family expectations increase temporarily. Being aware of when you're temporarily stretched and how long you're able to maintain the temporary change can help you plan how to get through it.

- *Knowing your limits for the long haul.* What's okay for you over time? Are you okay with sending work e-mail from home so you can get home earlier? Do you want to meet work expectations but let go of the long hours required to be a superstar?

- *Planning for specific problems that stress you out.* We all have specific things that stress us out, such as pet peeves, being late, or misplacing something. Knowing yours and arranging to take special care that those limits aren't pushed will reduce your stress.

- *Addressing limits when crossed.* Don't ignore times when you are spread too thin or when you're pushed into circumstances that are uncomfortable. Tell people when your limits are stretched and adopt an attitude of problem solving.

There is no one way to balance every demand in your life. However, paying attention to your limits can help reduce stress and keep life more manageable.

Wrap-Up

Your response to the stressors in your life has an impact on the intensity of your stress response and the amount of chronic stress in your life. The strategies in this chapter are designed to help you make sustainable changes and to improve the quality of your life.

Reducing your stress levels requires that you actively manage your life. Changes that you make can be difficult, at first, but it is possible to change how you cope and thus lower your stress levels, even in the midst of difficult circumstances.

With practice and attention, you can make long-lasting changes. The potential long-term gains, including improvements in both mental and physical well-being, are worth it.

References

Adam, T. C., and E. Epal. 2007. Stress, eating and the reward system. *Physiology and Behavior* 91:449–458.

Alberti, R. E., and M. L. Emmons. 1978. *Your Perfect Right: A Guide to Assertive Behavior.* Atascadero, CA: Impact Publishers.

Barker, L. L. 1971. *Listening Behavior.* Upper Saddle River, NJ: Prentice Hall.

Baumeister, R. F., and M. R. Leary. 1995. The need to belong: Desire for interpersonal attachments as fundmental human motivation. *Psychological Bulletin* 117(3):497–529.

Beck, A., and G. Emery. 2005. *Anxiety Disorders and Phobias: A Cognitive Perspective.* New York: Basic Books.

Beck, A., A. J. Rush, B. F. Shaw, and G. Emery. 1979. *Cognitive Therapy of Depression.* New York: The Guilford Press.

Carmody, J., and R. A. Baer. 2007. Relationships between mindfulness practice and levels of mindfulness, medical and psychological symptoms and well-being in a mindfulness-based stress reduction program. *Journal of Behavioral Medicine* 31:23–33.

Creswell, J. D., M. Baldwin, N. I. Eisenberger, and M. D. Lieberman. 2007. Neural correlates of dispositional mindfulness during affect labeling. *Psychosomatic Medicine* 69:560–565.

Crews, D. J., and D. M. Landers. 1987. Meta-analytic review of aerobic fitness and reactivity to psychosocial stressors. *Medicine and Science in Sports and Exercise* 19(5):114–120.

Davidson, R. J., J. Kabat-Zinn, J. Schumacher, M. Rosenkranz, D. Muller, S. F. Santorelli, F. Urbanowski, A. Harrington, K. Bonus, and J. F. Sheridan. 2003. Alterations in brain and immune function produced by mindfulness meditation. *Psychosomatic Medicine* 65:564–570.

DeLongis, A., R. Lazarus, and S. Folkman. 1988. The impact of daily stress on health and mood: Psychological and social resources as mediators. *Journal of Personality and Social Psychology* 54(3):486–495.

Dias-Ferreira, E., J. C. Sousa, I. Melo, P. Morgado, A. R. Mesquita, J. J. Cerqueira, R. M. Costa, and N. Sousa. 2009. Chronic stress causes frontostriatal reorganization and affects decision-making. *Science* 325:621–625.

Ellis, A., and R. A. Harper. 1975. *A New Guide to Rational Living*. Englewood Cliffs, NJ: Prentice Hall.

Epal, E., R. Lapidus, B. McEwen, and K. Brownell. 2001. Stress may add bite to appetite in women: A laboratory study of stress-induced cortisol and eating behavior. *Psychoneuroendocrinology* 26(1):37–49.

Fox, K. 1999. The influence of physical activity on mental well-being. *Public Health Nutrition* 2:411–418.

Gilovich, T., E. Pronin, and L. Ross. 2004. Objectivity in the eye of the beholder: Divergent perceptions of bias in self versus others. *Psychological Review* 111(3):781–799.

Goleman, D. 1977. *The Meditative Mind: The Varieties of Meditative Experience*. New York: Dutton.

Greenberg, J., T. Pyszczynski, and S. Solomon. 1982. The self-serving attributional bias: Beyond self-presentation. *Journal of Experimental Social Psychology* 18(1):56–67.

Grossman, P., L. Niemann, S. Schmidt, and H. Walach. 2004. Mindfulness-based stress reduction and health benefits: A meta-analysis. *Journal of Psychosomatic Research* 57:35–43.

Holmes, T., and R. Rahe. 1967. The Holmes-Rahe life stress inventory. *Journal of Psychosomatic Research* 11:216, Table 3.

Kabat-Zinn, J. 2003. Mindfulness-based interventions in context: Past, present, and future. *Clinical Psychology: Science and Practice* 10(2):144–156.

Kleinke, C. L., T. R. Peterson, and T. R. Rutledge. 1998. Effects of self-generated facial expressions on mood. *Journal of Personality and Social Psychology* 74:272–279.

Krause, E. D., T. Mendelson, and T. R. Lynch. 2003. Childhood emotional invalidation and adult psychological distress: The mediating role of emotional inhibition. *Child Abuse & Neglect* 27(2):199–213.

Kris-Etherton, P. M., W. S. Harris, and L. J. Appel (for the AHA Nutrition Committee). 2003. Omega-3 fatty acids and cardiovascular disease: New recommendations from the American Heart Association. *Arteriosclerosis, Thrombosis, and Vascular Biology* 23:151–152.

Lambert, N. M., and F. D. Fincham. 2011. Expressing gratitude to a partner leads to more relationship maintenance behavior. *Emotion* 11(1):52–60.

Lazarus, R. S. 1999. *Stress and Emotion: A New Synthesis.* New York: Springer.

Lepore, S. J. 1997. Expressive writing moderates the relation between intrusive thoughts and depressive symptoms. *Journal of Personality and Social Psychology* 73(5):1030–1037.

Lepore, S., J. D. Ragan, and S. Jones. 2000. Talking facilitates cognitive-emotional processes of adaptation to an acute stressor. *Journal of Personality and Social Psychology* 78(3):499–508.

Lieberman, D. A. 1990. *Learning: Behavior and Cognition.* Belmont, CA: Wadsworth.

Linehan, M. M. 1993a. *Cognitive Behavioral Treatment of Borderline Personality Disorder.* New York: Guilford Press.

Linehan, M. M. 1993b. *Skills Training Manual for Treating Borderline Personality Disorder.* New York: Guilford Press.

McEwen, B. S. 2007. Physiology and neurobiology of stress and adaptation: Central role of the brain. *Physiological Reviews* 87:873–904.

McKay, M., M. Davis, and P. Fanning. 2009. *Messages: The Communication Skills Book*. Oakland, CA: New Harbinger.

McMullen, J., D. Barnes-Holmes, Y. Barnes-Holmes, I. Stewart, C. Luciano, and A. Cochrane. 2008. Acceptance versus distraction: Brief instructions, metaphors and exercises in increasing tolerance for self-delivered electric shocks. *Behavior Research and Therapy* 46(1):122–129.

Melamed, S., A. Shirom, S. Toker, and I. Shapira. 2006. Burnout and risk of type 2 diabetes: A prospective study of apparently healthy employed persons. *Psychosomatic Medicine* 68:863–869.

Miller, G. E., S. Cohen, and A. K. Ritchie. 2002. Chronic psychological stress and the regulation of pro-inflammatory cytokines: A glucocorticoid-resistance model. *Health Psychology* 21(6):531–541.

Ophir, E., C. Nass, and A. D. Wagner. 2009. Cognitive control in media multitaskers. *Proceedings of the National Academy of Sciences of The United States of America. 106*:15583–15587.

Pennebaker, J. W., M. Colder, and L. K. Sharp. 1990. Accelerating the coping process. *Journal of Personality and Social Psychology* 58(3):528–537.

Plutchik, R. 1980. *Emotion: A Psychoevolutionary Synthesis*. New York: Harper and Row.

Roseman, I. J., C. Wiest, and T. S. Swartz. 1994. Phenomenology, behaviors, and goals differentiate discrete emotions. *Journal of Personality and Social Psychology* 67(2):206–221.

Salmon, P. 2001. Effects of physical exercise on anxiety, depression, and sensitivity to stress: A unifying theory. *Clinical Psychology Review* 21(1):33–61.

Sapolsky, R. M. 2004. *Why Zebras Don't Get Ulcers: The Acclaimed Guide to Stress, Stress-Related Diseases, and Coping*. New York: Henry Holt.

Taylor, S. E., L. C. Klein, B. P. Lewis, T. L. Gruenewald, R. A. R. Gurung, and J. A. Updegraff. 2000. Biobehavioral responses to stress in females: Tend-and-befriend, not fight-or-flight. *Psychology Review* 107(3):411–429.

Thich Nhat Hanh. 1991. *Peace Is Every Step: The Path of Mindfulness in Everyday Life*. New York: Bantam Books.

Updegraff, J. A., R. C. Silver, and A. Holman. 2008. Searching for and finding meaning in collective trauma: Results from a national longitudinal study on the 9/11 terrorist attacks. *Journal of Personality and Social Psychology* 95(3):709–722.

Warda, G., and R. A. Bryant. 1998. Cognitive bias in acute stress disorder. *Behaviour Research and Therapy* 36(12):1177–1183.

Winbush, N. Y., C. R. Gross, and M. J. Kreitzer. 2007. The effects of mindfulness-based stress reduction on sleep disturbance: A systematic review. *Explore: The Journal of Science and Healing* 3(6):585–591.

Christy Matta, MA, has worked in mental health for over twenty years as a clinician, trainer, and administrator, specializing in the treatment of emotion dysregulation and behavioral problems. She is trained in dialectical behavior therapy (DBT) and has provided training and clinical supervision to DBT programs, staff, and clinicians. She has presented nationally on the topic of DBT and participated in the design and clinical supervision of DBT residential programs, including a program that went on to win the American Psychiatric Association's Gold Award.

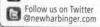